THE TAO OF STARTUPS

创业道

A GUIDEBOOK FOR YOUR ENTREPRENEURIAL LIFE

James LaLonde

Copyright © 2018

James LaLonde and Winston's Will Publishing

ISBN:

ISBN-13: 978-1-7328368-1-5

Get all the free reference and supplementary materials as well as more information on startups and the author:

www.startuptaobook.com

DEDICATION

I want to thank Henry, Emily, Luke, Terry and all the entrepreneurs I have worked with, shared war stories with and mentored over the years. You know who you are.

I am extremely happy to share this book with all readers. Personally, I am an avid reader and I read (and re-read) somewhere between 200 and 300 books a year. Without a doubt the book I have read the most often is the "Tao Te Ching" by Lao Tzu. I find the words in its pages have helped me get through the ups and downs of the startup life and more importantly helped me keep things in perspective. I have selected a few of my favorite passages from the book to precede each chapter. All the quotes used in this book are from: *Mitchell, Stephen. Tao Te Ching: A New English Version. Harper Perennial.*

TABLE OF CONTENTS

Introduction

Chapter 1 - The Basics

Chapter 2 - The Idea

Chapter 3- The Elevator Pitch

Chapter 4- The Co-Founders

Chapter 5- The MVP

Chapter 6- The Pitch Deck

Chapter 7- The Funding Options

Chapter 8- Splitting the Equity

Chapter 9- The Valuation

Chapter 10- The Investor Meetings

Chapter 11- The Due Diligence

Conclusion

About The Author

Bibliography

INTRODUCTION

This book came from a presentation called "The Tao of Startups" I gave to an audience of entrepreneurs and investors on March 23, 2018, at the China Accelerator 8x8 Event in Beijing. As the other seven presenters, I was given only 8 minutes to provide inspiration and guidance to the latest batch of startup founders at China Accelerator. This particular time I decided to condense fifteen years of doing startups and mentoring other startup founders into a coherent presentation that would help all of them get through the tremendous uphill climb they were about to embark upon. The inherent challenge of doing something as ridiculous as boiling down everything I knew to its bare essence in order to meet the time requirement ended up really inspiring me. The purpose of the talk was to take the audience through the entire "cycle" of creating a startup and discuss what is important (and what is not important) during each phase. Doing a startup is difficult and can be extremely stressful. It can also be extremely fulfilling. I wanted to lead the audience through a "guided meditation" of sorts to put them in the proper frame of mind for doing a startup—to look at the process from a holistic point of view.

Writing this book in Beijing, China, I am literally at the epicenter of the new startup world. And it is a post-Silicon Valley startup world where currently 47% of startup funds worldwide are directed at China. Right now it is estimated that more than 12,000 startups are created each day in China. Beijing has established itself as the new birthplace of unicorns as more have been created here than any other place in the world outside of Silicon Valley. And with the successful government/private sector cooperation that has resulted in the epic growth story that is China of the last 30 years, this startup activity is actively supported by the central government in Beijing which is laser-focused on transforming China from the "world's factory" to the "world's leader in innovation".

While I have lived and traveled all over the world, including a decade in Silicon Valley, as a serial entrepreneur and a person who genuinely derives great personal satisfaction and intellectual stimulation in taking an idea and turning it into an actual business, there is no place on earth than I would rather be in this specific point in history. The buzz in the air and the opportunities seem boundless from where I sit right now writing this in Beijing.

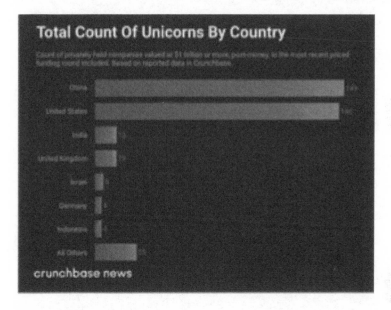

That said, this is not a book about China or the startup scene here. This is a book that is about the reality that the issues startups face, for the most part, are universal and applicable everywhere. Over the last three years in my association with

China Accelerator and on my own have mentored hundreds of Chinese and non-Chinese founders both in China and around the world. What amazes me is that the concepts, strategies and the advice contained in this book are not specific to any particular country, locale or language. Startups all over the world face the same issues. With China beginning its golden age of startups and innovation, the wisdom, learnings and best practices of Silicon Valley and startups the world over are more in demand than ever here in China. In some way, I hope to help entrepreneurs avoid some of the common pitfalls and encourage them to be more thorough and thoughtful about crucial issues in the early stages of a startup. Because at the end of the day while everyone can and should learn from failure, it is the business success that will ultimately put food on the table, send kids to school and fund the future. If a few more startups are successful due to some of the learnings I share in this book, then I will have accomplished what I have set out to do by writing it.

Reed Hoffman, Silicon Valley investor, co-founder of PayPal and LinkedIn says, *"Entrepreneurship is a life idea, not a strictly business one; a global idea, not a strictly American one."*

James LaLonde

Beijing, September 2018

Tao Te Ching 道德经 Verse 63

Act without doing;

work without effort.

Think of the small as large

and the few as many.

Confront the difficult

while it is still easy;

accomplish the great task

by a series of small acts.

The Master never reaches for the great;

thus he achieves greatness.

When he runs into a difficulty,

he stops and gives himself to it.

He doesn't cling to his own comfort;

thus problems are no problem for him.

1

THE BASICS

What is a Startup, really?

A startup is a chance for you to learn, learn an awful lot, in an intense way. You will have many moments of success, but more than anything you will learn about failure. Like Thomas Edison toiling away in his laboratory, tirelessly carrying out one failed experiment after the other, you and your co-founders will learn from all the small failures and obstacles you face. How you deal with failure and how you use what you learn to provide the motivation and sustenance you need to continue moving forward will teach you a lot about yourself.

Unlike school, startups operate in the Darwinian real world. More likely than not your startup will fail. According to CB Insights, more than 70% of startups fail within twenty months of their first funding (average $1.3 million of funding raised). This book was written for all those who are doing and thinking of doing startups that intend to make the most of the life experience doing a startup can give you. Think of it this way, two years doing a startup will provide you with infinitely more experience as a business person than spending two years getting an MBA. This book is intended to equip you with the basic knowledge you need to successfully navigate through your startup odyssey.

If you are going to do a startup, let's make sure you know what a startup is. This is non-trivial and the first thing you need to understand. Though it may be excellent "practice" and a fun way to experience some aspects of being an entrepreneur, a startup is not opening a lemonade stand or a car washing business you do on the weekends. A startup is not a part-time comedy stand up routine you do at a comedy club, either. Being an actor, skilled craftsperson, or artist is also not a startup for the purposes of this book. A startup is not anything you can do by yourself. Why? You ask.

The answer is that the concept of scalability is inextricably intertwined with the modern definition of a startup. And that is indeed the case with this book.

A one-person business, while it may provide a good income, is not generally scalable. Many service businesses (unless they can be franchised) are not scalable either. This category includes restaurants, various shops, concierge services. These are what we call "small business," and while these types of businesses have been the backbone of the world economy for centuries, they are by definition, local in nature and scope. In today's inter-connected, fast-paced world these types of businesses are finding it harder to survive and certainly are not the center of innovation in the economy anymore.

Innovation is another concept that is inextricably connected with a successful startup. The product or service delivered by the startup must at its core have some level of innovation—something that is, or is done differently or in a new, fresh way in order to have a chance to become highly successful and grow quickly.

A Startup   # A Scaleup

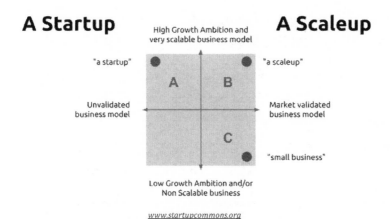

High Growth Ambition and
very scalable business model

"a startup"   "a scaleup"

A   B

Unvalidated   Market validated
business model   business model

C

"small business"

Low Growth Ambition and/or
Non Scalable business

www.startupcommons.org

A startup is a venture that is initiated by its founders around an idea or a problem with a potential for significant business opportunity and impact. Often the actual development starts even before that with a search for an idea or an important problem worth solving and building a committed founding team aligned with a shared vision to make that vision into reality.

The aim of the initial founder(s) is to establish a committed co-founder team with necessary skills and abilities to be able to validate the initial problem/solution fit and product/market fit, before scaling it to a significant company and self-sustained business.

So in addition to the innovation process itself, from idea to value generating product and business model, startups also need to have a strong and committed founding team and develop both of these together into a real growth business and organization that captures the value being created as a great company.

A great company is a self sustaining entity that is no longer dependent on any single individual or other organization, where all necessary knowledge, values, strategies, intellectual property (IPR), etc. are permanently embedded into its existence in a way that it can continue to operate, improve and build value for customers, shareholders and other key stakeholders, while remaining financially stable by the value of solutions and products it creates.

Entrepreneurship vs. Startups vs. SME's vs. Scaleups

Few things are as important as common understanding and definitions. Without knowing precisely what specific terms mean, and how they apply to given situations, very little discourse on startup or ecosystems development can take place. In developing startups and startup ecosystems, there are still many terms that are misunderstood or misused.

Beyond defining it as a "newly established business," the term "startup" is not really well defined out there in the real world. For the purposes of this book, a startup is defined as a company formed by two or more entrepreneurs (called "co-founders) to do something new or in a completely new way in order to satisfy a customer need that has not existed or not been serviced well by existing companies. The general essence of a startup is that it is a (eventually) highly scalable, fast-growing company that has the ability to create a substantial market presence and therefore market value in a very short period of time.

en·tre·pre·neur

/ˌäntrəprəˈnər/ ◄)

noun

a person who organizes and operates a business or businesses, taking on greater than normal financial risks in order to do so.

An entrepreneur is an individual; a startup is an entrepreneurial team that comes together to build a business. However, the media often highlights individual entrepreneurs over the team which has a blurring effect on how startups are perceived. Also, a startup is not simply a smaller version of a big company, but an "organization formed to search for a repeatable and scalable business model." A startup, by definition, is in the process of creation and growth, where growth is not only measured merely by traditional business terms like revenue or profit, but also by market share, number of active users etc. For example, unlike more traditional businesses, a startup's success might be measured on a free product or service where no revenue is being generated at the moment.

For these reasons, startups can also not be categorized only by the size of the company, ie. SME, Mid Cap or Large corporation, or by their resources, i.e., number of people, profits, assets, etc., or the age of the company. Startups are commonly considered to be anything from few co-founding people and an idea, in some cases even without having registered a company yet, - to company's that are several years old with tens or even hundreds of people, regardless of making or not any profits or revenue yet for several years. That said, sometimes startups also prefer not to call or see themselves as startups when it suits their needs, like in some cases when they want to appear more stable or mature, i.e., in the eyes of a significant customer.

To mix things up, even more, there is another related and relatively new term that has started to emerge in recent years that is "scaleup." While this can be logically described to be a company at the scaling phase, there is another aspect to consider. It is a term that is not limited for a startup that has reached the scaling phase, but can be also used for an older company that have found a new scaling mode as a result of new product/service and/or new owners with new growth ambitions and/or business model.

At the same time, due to the fast development of certain ecosystems in technology, the internet, software, open source concepts, API's, app stores and other platforms, crowdfunding, ICOs, etc. startups are no longer as dependent on initial capital injections in the form of venture capital or angel funding to create a "funding round." So while a successful funding round can be one type of positive indicator along with other validation signals, it should not be interpreted as a measure of actual success, but just as a single milestone.

Today, more than ever, choosing the external investor route is an "option" rather than a "must." That said, it makes sense to build the business also to be investable, to have that option available in case that strategy would turn out to be the right one to choose at some point. Anything an investor would look for in a startup is also good for business in general as well.

All things considered, the topic of "investors" and "search for investments" are disproportionately over-represented in startup ecosystem support targets compared to all other things that are critical factors for the success of a startup.

Why do a Startup?

To build a successful startup you will be living in a world where you are being pulled a thousand different ways: investors that want more sales and profitability, users who want more features and attention, people who want to learn from you, people who want to sabotage you, people who want to hate on you. All of these forces will work to utilize the already scarce resources you have (e.g., time, energy, talent, luck and money). You need to become good at focusing and prioritizing. Maintaining your focus in the midst of chaos is a learned, not genetic trait. Moreover, you have to keep your eye on the goal and the big picture while executing in the realm of minutiae.

In your startup life, there will always be another milestone that is further out and harder to reach. You must develop ways to avoid finding yourself in a chronic place of stress because that is not sustainable and certainly not healthy in a physical nor emotional sense. That is why this book is called the "Tao of Startups." Integration of Daoist concepts into my work and life to obtain "work/life harmony" (this is the term Jeff Bezos uses instead of "work/life balance" which he says is a "debilitating phrase" because it implies there's a strict trade-off) have sustained me through multiple successful startups.

> *If you think something is hard, it will BE hard. If you believe you can do something YOU can. It is really all up to you and your perception of reality.* - James LaLonde

If you were planning to climb Mount Everest and intend to return home to tell the tale, you would train and prepare diligently, sometimes for years, and you'd bring along a capable support team because it is well known that such a task is incredibly hard. Understanding from the outset that startups are hard and then properly preparing your mind and your expectations so that you see an overarching reason for what you are undertaking is essential. This is, unfortunately, not the mindset the majority of people doing startups today bring to the table.

More often than not, people do startups on a whim, a casual discussion over beers shared. This is the "Hollywood version" of how startups are born. In this book, I will take you step-by-step through how to not only choose your co-founders but how to discuss and settle delicate matters such as share ownership, vesting, performance target setting and domains of control. Unlike affairs of the heart, with a startup, you absolutely need a prenuptial agreement.

By underestimating and not seriously contemplating the difficulty and complexity involved, most people start out with loosely aligned, and intrinsically flawed, expectations. Or, much worse, the founders start out quite literally with widely varied expectations. These situations are where a positive mindset— essential to have in abundance in all startup teams--can backfire on you. The founders imagine it will be easier and it ends up being much harder than they ever imagined. It logically follows that expecting it to be hard, but eminently possible, is something that needs to be commonly understood amongst the founder team.

Jessica Livingston of Y Combinator once said: "Startups are an entirely new level of hard because they contain so many different varieties of hard." VCs have funded math wizards, rocket scientists, triathletes, Rhodes Scholars, etc. All of these people are used to succeeding. But guess what? They fail at startups. Why? Because succeeding at a startup is fundamentally different from succeeding in work or graduate school.

I admire Winston Churchill. A born leader, he had two traits which I particularly endorse. One he was not afraid to speak his mind and give his opinion (in both the U.K. House of Parliment and in the pages of his numerous books). Being at odds with current public opinion often had a detrimental effect on his political career. However, he was only a politician as a means to an end, as a platform to affect change. The second aspect, and perhaps the main reason he looms large as a historical figure is his "never give up" attitude. This trait permeated the very essence of his being. A successful entrepreneur needs to either have or learn these traits as startups are hard in many ways that have nothing to do with the product or service itself. For example tolerance for ambiguity, co-founder stress, managing people (easier said than done!), lack of sleep, pressure from many different directions and even loneliness.

That said, you can't focus on the downside. That will prevent you from ever starting. Even though I have planned well (better for each successive startup) in the end, I am never able to conceptualize precisely how hard it actually is, what parts of the business prove to be difficult (and easy!). One important thing you can do from the outset is to realize the eventual success of your startups is beyond your control. Vinod Khosla, co-founder of Sun Microsystems and founder of Khosla Ventures, said: "In my decades of encouraging entrepreneurs and innovation, I have learned that an entrepreneur probably only controls approximately 30 to 40-percent of the factors that affect their success. Competitors and environmental circumstances often make up the rest."

Regarding your startup, it can be helpful to break things down into those that you can fully control, things you can have some control over, and things that you don't have any control over, for example:

- Things you can 100% control: burn rate and how much you choose to work.
- Things you have some control over: people you hire; growth rate; retention; and revenue.
- Things you have no control over: competitors; technology shifts; personal crises that impact your employees.

Spend less time worrying about things you can't control and more time being proactive about the things you can. It can be a great relief to have permission to look at reality and say "We will try our best, but there will always be variables beyond our control."

All over the world, Alcoholics Anonymous has a fantastic track record of curing people of arguably the most challenging addiction a human can face: chronic alcoholism. At the beginning of each session, they recite the Serenity Prayer. Even if you are not religious and not an addict you can benefit from this powerful prose:

God grant me the serenity to accept the things I cannot change; courage to change the things I can; and wisdom to know the difference.

If you break it down, it is two basic tenets:

1. To keep your sanity focus your energy on the things that are in your power to control, not the things beyond your control
2. Take one day at a time. Focus on succeding at something each day and tallying up your small successes on a daily basis as taken together over a long period they result in a larger, tangible success

This powerful combination allows you to rid your life of unnecessary stress and avoid procrastination. Unmanageable stress and procrastination are lethal to startups.

Your time on this earth is limited. The Serenity Prayer helps you avoid focusing on things you don't have direct control over. But you really do need to take ownership of the things you can control. A big one is how you spend your time. You shouldn't waste time flitting from startup idea to startup idea. To avoid this, long ago I made a habit of immediately documenting every business idea I have. First I wrote them down, then I carried a voice recorder with me. For the last decade, I have used a smartphone and Evernote (I have nearly 20,000 notes stored with them). That typically adds up to a hundred or so business ideas in the course of a year. I consider each one (many for only a few minutes, some for days/weeks) and at the end of the day end up acting on approximately 1 in 500. That is less than 0.2 percent of the total. I am not saying I am typical. Most people have fewer ideas than myself; some have many more. Even fewer ever bother to write them down. What I am saying is that by the time I have decided to test or actually act on an idea I have spent quite a bit of time not only thinking it through but analyzing it through my "Opportunity Cost Filter."

The New Oxford American Dictionary defines "opportunity cost" as *the loss of potential gain from other alternatives when one alternative is chosen*. This simple concept has powerful implications.

When I was in college (Economics was my major), we studied the opportunity costs of using a factory to produce one type of product versus another one. If a production line can only be used for one product at a time you need to be very careful about how you utilize it to produce what. I learned formulas to do calculations for these types of scenarios. The only equivalent I have found in my "real world" is allocating software developers on tasks. If you have only a few good programmers, which projects you put them on can make a big difference. From an investment scenario, returns you could have earned if you invested the money in one financial instrument versus another also applies. Buying 1,000 shares in company A costing $10 each might eventually sell for $12 a share, netting a profit of $2,000. However, lets suppose that during the same period, company B rose in value from $10 a share to $15. In this scenario, investing $10,000 in company A netted a yield of $2,000, while the same amount invested in company B would have netted $5,000. The $3,000 difference is the opportunity cost of choosing company A over company B.

More simply put, opportunity cost is inextricably linked with the notion nearly every decision requires a trade-off. We live in a finite world; you can't be in two places at once. That means if you choose one restaurant to eat dinner tonight, you can't choose another—not tonight at least.

Right now, you are reading this book when you could have been golfing, or writing, or exercising, or doing charity work, or using drugs, or learning a new skill, or watching a movie or on a date with your girlfriend or wife. For the factors you have control over, your life is the sum culmination of your past decisions. That is the layman's definition of opportunity cost. The economists make it seem complicated, but think about it in another way, by pondering the following real-world decisions:

- What if Mark Zuckerberg didn't drop out of Harvard and commit to move to and pursue Facebook full time in Silicon Valley?
- What if Walt Disney never decided to open an animation studio?
- What if Thomas Edison gave up on perfecting on the light bulb after he failed after the first 100 or 1,000 prototypes?
- What if Steve Jobs had decided to never return to Apple and stick with Next Computer?

So if each startup you do will take at least 3-10 years of your life in a highly intense way, you can only do a few in your lifetime. Therefore considering the opportunity cost of doing a startup (including which startup), getting married, starting a family, etc., are all serious considerations.

Ultimately, doing a startup is a tremendous leap of faith. You can build an amazing team, get real product traction, get funded by investors, solve real problems for your users, but, even still, it might not get you the outcome you want. On some level, you have to be okay with that, because that is the mathematical reality. This is precisely why it is so important to work on something that you really care deeply about — work that is personally meaningful to you — because, then, even if you fail to become a unicorn, you still succeed in life

Also, remember that your startup, which you are so involved with today is but one chapter of your life, one part of your personal narrative. You are a founder of a startup, but you are also a partner, son or daughter, father or mother, friend, and student. Only you have the power to decide what your startup's success or failure will mean in the context of the larger story of your life.

What motivates people to do Startups?

Understand your and your co-founder's motivations. Write them down and share them. In my experience, you need to set your expectations on what you intend to learn via doing your startup. Since you will always learn valuable (if not extremely hard) lessons when doing a startup, you should focus on what you intend to learn. Chances are your first startup will not be successful, but if you apply the learning to your second startup or your life post-startup, you will always have something valuable to show for it.

The financial rewards motivate lots of people, and it is true that most people who "make the big bucks" did it by starting (and selling off) a company they founded.

Activities that propelled people to the Top 400 "Rich List" in the US (data from the U.S. Internal Revenue Service)

- 13.6% stock market investing (mostly high profile traders and investors)

- 8.6% working as the CEO (or other highly paid role) in a company

- 6.6% holding interest-bearing investments (people who likely inherited the money)

- 65.7% sale of ownership in a business or partnership (e.g., selling or IPO'ing a company you co-founded)

So while making a fortune is indeed possible if your company is successful, being a startup founder is certainly not the only way to get there. Being an early employee of a promising startup is certainly an option for those who have a smaller appetite for risk than being a co-founder entails.

Motivator	Myth	Reality
Financial Success	Founding a company and having a large equity stake is the best way to become independently wealthy	Being and early employee of a successful startup is a more surefire way to become independently wealthy
Social Impact	Running an entire company is the only way to have an impact	Running an established product line or team can allow you to make a real difference
Lifestyle	Celebrity-like	Hard work, high stress, inability to separate yourself from the company

"The 100th engineer at Facebook had a way better financial outcome than the vast majority of entrepreneurs" co-founder of Facebook and Asana, Dustin Moskovitz.

The reality of being a startup founder is different from the widely-held perception--it is far less glamorous. Let's look at some common things that motivate people to become entrepreneurs in the first place.

Very few (less than 1%) startups achieve unicorns status and make their founders ultra-wealthy. While you should set ambitious goals for yourself and your startup, the reality is that just surviving and creating a sustainable, growing business is the second most likely outcome. The first most likely outcome is failure.

THE VENTURE CAPITAL FUNNEL

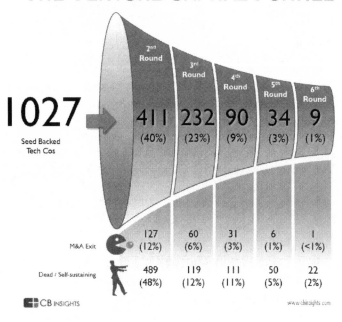

	2nd Round	3rd Round	4th Round	5th Round	6th Round
1027 Seed Backed Tech Cos	411 (40%)	232 (23%)	90 (9%)	34 (3%)	9 (1%)
M&A Exit	127 (12%)	60 (6%)	31 (3%)	6 (1%)	1 (<1%)
Dead / Self-sustaining	489 (48%)	119 (12%)	111 (11%)	50 (5%)	22 (2%)

CB INSIGHTS   www.cbinsights.com

So before you start a company, take some time to ensure your personal goals are compatible with your desire to create a startup. Depending on where you are with your career, there are many reasons for you seriously consider being an early startup employee versus a co-founder

Comparing startup funding data compiled by CB Insights with statistics taken from the National College Athletes Association (NCAA) study and draft data from 2017, it is almost twice as likely for you to become a Major League Baseball (MLB) player than be a co-founder in successful startup that reaches the fifth round of VC and institutional investment.

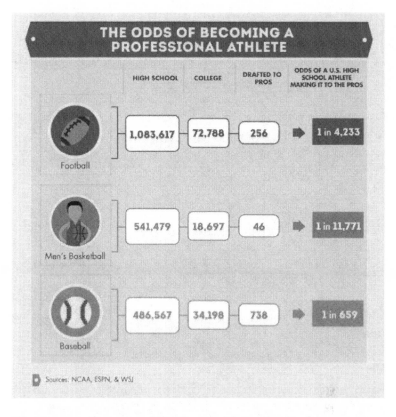

The chances that a small business will survive for five years in the United States are about 35%. However, the individuals who open such businesses do not believe the statistics apply to them. A survey found that American entrepreneurs tend to think they are in a promising line of business: their average estimate of the chances of success for "any business like yours" was 60%—almost double the true value. The bias was more glaring when people assessed the odds of their own venture. Fully 81% of the entrepreneurs put their personal odds of success at 7 out of 10 or higher, and 33% said their chance of failing was zero. - Daniel Kahneman, "Thinking Fast and Slow"

If you have read this far, you may feel like you want to jump in. Great! That is what this book is for, in the next ten chapters I will break down for you the key aspects you need to dig into as you go through the startup process.

All startups go through a series of phases in their early development and while some may be longer or shorter depending on your team, market conditions and the type of company you are starting; it is important that you visualize your progress and know exactly which phase you are in at any given point of time.

Startupcommons.org has created a wonderfully useful graphic called the "Startup Development Phases", and through the years I have used it extensively in my mentoring work as well as in my startups.

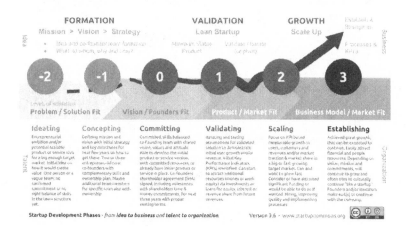

The powerful beauty of this graphic is that it is self-explanatory and real-world tested. Please take a minute now to read through it. This book is intended to get your through to phase 2 and past the rocky shoals that sink most startups before they get a chance to grow in phase 3. The main reason I wrote this book is that most of the literature in the marketplace today focuses on phase 3. In fact, until Eric Ries wrote "The Lean Startup" which focuses primarily on phase 1 and 2, there were relatively few useful books on those phases. Lately, through my mentoring activities, I find that the key issues with new startup founders today is thinking through phases -2 to 1. These are the phases that are often overlooked or rushed through and therefore end up causing the bulk of startup failures.

Are you ready? Following are the 10 things you need to do to be successful in doing a startup:

Over the years I have found myself going back to the following "reminder to self" list that ensures myself and the founding teams I am a part of or the ones I mentor stay focused. The list is in somewhat of a chronological order but not exactly. I suggest you keep these points "top of mind" when doing your startup.

1. Choose good co-founders.

Selecting co-founder(s) is your most important decision and will impact whether the startup succeeds or fails more than any other decision in the formative early years of the startup. Spend time on it and get it right. This topic is covered in Chapter 4.

2. Set a date and launch fast.

Once you think you have the founding team together, immediately get yourselves locked into a room with a whiteboard and map out your MVP (see Chapter 5 on how to do this). Then do a gut check and give yourselves a date to launch the product. This date needs to be a fixed date, and you must not slip. Not only will this be the first test of your team's ability to execute within time and monetary constraints, but it will give you the focus you need to put the wheels of the startup in motion. Every minute you waste not building the product/service that you are going to put in front of customers is jeopardizing your future success. The process of scoping, building and launching the product will tell you most of what you need to know about the team, the market and your users. You will not get it right the first time, but it is incredibly important that you get the product launched. The vast majority of startups end as ideas. Shipping your product/service immediately places you and your team ahead of all the wantrepreneurs!

3. Learn and iterate post launch

Make sure you measure the success of your product post-launch and how your users are using (or not using) it. Clean up some of the messy bits that didn't get done by launch time. Understand the flow and how the users are interacting with the product. Hopefully, you have charged something for the product, understand your sales and value proposition post-launch. Decide when you will ship an update and what features will be included and which not.

4. Forget the mass market. Work hard to make your early users love you

You had to cut corners to get the product out the door quickly. That is why it is called the Minimum Viable Product (MVP). There will be users who are not satisfied with the product, and you need to take the time to understand why. But don't overlook those users who bought your first version and are using it. Instead, give them excellent service and learn as much as you can from them. Over time you can make the product that will appeal to the less zealous users but for now treat your early customers well.

5. Don't compromise on customer service

Make it a point to answer every query and satisfy every customer (even if it means returning their money) Make sure your customer service is not just good, but surprisingly good. Go out of your way to make your users happy. They'll be appreciative and even more importantly, will be invested in your startup's success. In the early days of a startup, it is crucial to offer customer service on a level that wouldn't scale long term, because it's a way of learning about your users.

6. Decide what matters and measure it

If revenue is most important, measure it on a daily basis. If customer satisfaction is most important, then find a metric that serves as a proxy for that and measure it. Don't have lots of targets and things you measure. Just know that as your business and team grows, what you measure will change. Measure what is important for your success, right now and make sure everyone sees it and discusses it. Deciding what you care about is important and can be a double-edged sword. This is because it has an impact on culture. What the founding team cares about (or doesn't care about) is reflected in everyone's daily activities. Also, the metric needs to be something the team can control. Just like watching the temperature outside can be useful and impact some decisions, it is certainly something no one person on the team can directly control or impact. Therefore it is meaningless as a company metric.

7. Create a culture of thrift.

Every dollar not spent is more time the company can keep its doors open before the product takes off. Even if you are VC-funded, every employee should spend money like it is coming out of his/her own pocket. Said another way, a "when in doubt, don't pull your wallet out" mentality will enable the company to be lean, iterate fast and not be beholden to a burn rate that could pre-maturely cripple it.

8. Get ramen profitable, quickly.

"Ramen profitable" means a startup makes just enough to pay the founders' living expenses. Having to worry about making rent and where you will sleep is not the kind of thing a founder building a company on a shoestring should need to worry about. It is just counterproductive. Also, being ramen profitable makes you more confident as a company and also changes your relationship with investors. It's also just great for morale. So make one of your early goals to get to ramen profitability ASAP.

9. Avoid distractions.

Distractions are like kryptonite for startups. They allow you to think you are doing fine when your core business is suffering, and your priorities are off. Far and away the worst distractions are those that pay money: day jobs, consulting, profitable side-projects. The startup may have more long-term potential, but you'll always interrupt working on it to answer calls from people paying you now. Unfortunately, fundraising is also a similar type of distraction, so do whatever you can to not be in a position of always needing to raise money.

10. Don't give up, stay positive.

With a startup, the highs are incredibly high, and the lows are extremely low. Even if you get demoralized, don't give up. Persevere! This is a unique thing about startups is that you can get really far if you don't give up. Most people never act on ideas and even those that do tend to give up as soon as they meet some resistance. There are a lot of people who couldn't become good pianists no matter how long they practiced. However, startups aren't like that. Sheer effort is usually enough, so long as you keep iterating on your idea. Deals and opportunities for your startup come and go. Build a "post-mortem" process into your team's collective thinking processes, so the learning is captured. Never forget that every lost deal or partnership that didn't pan out happened for a reason, some part within and some part outside your sphere of control. Remember to focus your effort on getting better instead of obsessing over "what could have been."

Tao Te Ching 道德经 Verse 41

When a superior man hears of the Tao, he immediately begins to embody it.

When an average man hears of the Tao, he half believes it, half doubts it.

When a foolish man hears of the Tao, he laughs out loud. If he didn't laugh, it wouldn't be the Tao.

Thus it is said: The path into the light seems dark, the path forward seems to go back, the direct path seems long, true power seems weak, true purity seems tarnished, true steadfastness seems changeable, true clarity seems obscure, the greatest art seems unsophisticated, the greatest love seems indifferent, the greatest wisdom seems childish.

The Tao is nowhere to be found. Yet it nourishes and completes all things.

2

THE IDEA

IT IS NOT ALL ABOUT THE IDEA.

In the startup world, there is a lot of talk about the original "idea" or the "big idea." Actually, the original idea is just a seed. It is a tiny thing that has a small amount of inherent potential. However, without the right combination of environmental factors (topsoil, water, sunlight, protection from animals, insects, adverse weather, etc.) it will not reach its potential. Moreover, if it does grow, an idea will often morph so much as to be unrecognizable. Just like the tree that grows large from a single seed does not in any way resemble the original seed; the idea looks very little like the final product. So, in a startup, it makes no sense to focus too much on the original idea or who had it first.

There is nothing new under the sun. You are not the first person to think of the idea, nor is it your first idea. The trick is to choose the idea you want to build a startup on, validate it properly and then EXECUTE. A startup is all about execution, not the original idea. But a bad idea is still bad!

So ideas are like seeds: over-produced, similar-looking, and the vast majority reach full potential due to lack of critical environmental factors.

History shows that most of our revered business icons built their success on the back of other people's ideas: it wasn't the McDonald brothers who built McDonald's into an empire, it was Ray Kroc who saw the potential for success in their operation and bought it from them. Steve Jobs of Apple had a tour of Xerox Parc and left convinced he knew where the future of personal computing was heading. He became obsessed, creating Lisa and the Macintosh and in the end, was fired from the company he co-founded. Google certainly was not the first search engine; it was just the last, best and most hungry and scrappy one. The likes of Zappos, Facebook, Uber, Airbnb were all examples of better execution of an idea someone else came up with first.

So it makes no sense to overly focus on the brilliance of the idea—an idea without execution is worthless. Nor should a founder intimidated by the fact that others may already be executing the same idea. Actually, if others are starting something similar, it only means that the time for the idea to be appropriately implemented on has finally come. The automotive industry holds numerous examples. Ferdinand Verbiest, a Jesuit missionary in China, built a steam-powered vehicle around 1672 as a gift for the Chinese Emperor. It was too small to carry a driver, but it was the first record of a working steam-powered vehicle. Just over a hundred years later, a steam-powered car was built by Nicolas-Joseph Cugnot in 1769. The idea of an automobile that was powered by a gasoline combustion engine (first built by Siegfried Marcus in 1870 and placed on a pushcart) that could be mass produced took another 150 years until the Ford Model T which debuted in 1913. While there have been more than 10,000 companies set up to create automobiles over the course of history, there remain less than 100 companies today doing so. That said, this could all change as automobiles switch powerplants. Recent startups like Tesla and several new Chinese automakers are a testament to the fact that it is not so much about the core idea as it is about execution and satisfying the customer. Time from idea to execution is much faster these days than it was in the early days of the automobile.

So a real entrepreneur is never dismayed because someone else is working on a similar idea. If instead, there are competitors, but they are struggling, it may be because they are too focused on the idea and not on execution or perfecting their fit to market and customer. Conversely, if there are no businesses with that idea, then it is possible that there is no market for it or the timing is not right. Investors see this all the time. If choosing between founders with amazing ideas but poor execution abilities and one founder with proven execution ability and a less than an earth-shattering idea, the smart bet is on the founder that can execute.

The takeaway is that if you think you have a great idea, find a team you think can execute on it, do an MVP, give yourself a finite runway to launch and test it on the market: if it works, develop it. If it doesn't, move on. If there are already competitors in the marketplace with the same idea and they're thriving, that proves there's a market. They are testing it for you. Take them on.

Share your ideas—don't keep them to yourself. You should have a circle of friends, acquaintances and even people you need that can serve as a sounding board for your ideas. In a given year I get 50 to 100 ideas. I always have five ideas on heavy rotation. The ideas that I am thinking about doing an MVP on. I also have another 20 or so that if I meet the right person, I will whip out and discuss. It makes no sense to hold on to an idea that you're never going to execute on. Who knows, it could be the seed of somebody else's success—and help make the ecosystem better for everyone.

Another key factor is embodied in Sequoia's famous question: Why now? Why is this the right time for this particular idea, and to start this specific company? Why wasn't it done two years ago, or why will two years into the future be too late? You should think about this for two reasons: it is important to answer this question honestly, so you don't waste several years of your life executing a great idea at the wrong time. Also, a smart investor will ask you this question. Think of how the Google guys answered it when there were so many search engines already on the market. This question will get you to the essence of your justification for the massive amount of time and effort you will put into your startup

One good rule of thumb that also answers the "why now?" question is if you're building something that you yourself need and want to use. You'll understand it much better than if you have to realize it by talking to customers to build the very first version. Think of a group of guys trying to build a website to sell custom-fit women's shoes. The learning curve is huge for them. If you don't want to use it yourself, and you're building something someone else needs, be cognizant that you're at a big disadvantage, and the only way to overcome it is to get extremely close to your customers. Try to work in their office, if you can, and if not, talk to them multiple times a day. This reminds me of my early days at Microsoft. As part of the sales team, we had to come into the office and boot up Microsoft Powerpoint 30 minutes before we planned to use it. We used the time to brew the coffee, talk shop and prepare for our calls. The program was just too slow on the Intel 286 processor PCs we had in the sales office. The developers in Redmond had no such issues as they developed the software on state of the art Intel 486 PCs. They also didn't use the product every day as we did and our customers more often than not had older PCs that made using the program impractical. We had to complain a lot and extremely loudly before Steve Ballmer finally mandated that all Powerpoint developers had to use Intel 286 PCs so they could "feel our pain" as part of the "Eat Your Own Dog Food" policy the company had recently implemented.

WHY EVERY COMPANY
SHOULD EAT ITS
OWN DOG FOOD

"Eat Your Own Dog Food" is a slang term that describes a company using its own products or services for its internal operations. In 1988, Microsoft executive Paul Maritz sent

Brian Valentine, test manager for Microsoft LAN Manager, an email entitled "Eating our own Dogfood," that challenged him to get all of Microsoft running on Microsoft LAN Manager (which later was replaced by functionality in Windows NT). From that email, the usage of the term spread like fire throughout the company. In early 1991, Dave Cutler's insistence on dogfooding in development of Windows NT with daily builds at Microsoft was key to its eventual adoption in the corporate IT world. As a result in 2005, after a tour of Microsoft's network operations center, Infoworld reported that "showed pretty much beyond a reasonable doubt that Microsoft does run its 20,000-plus node, international network on 99 percent Windows technology, including servers, workstations, and edge security". InfoWorld said that "Microsoft's use of Windows for its high-traffic operations tipped many doubters over to Windows' side of the fence."

Occam's Razor (or Ockham's Razor, also known as the Principle of Parsimony) is the idea that more straightforward explanations are, in general, better. That is, if you have two possible theories that fit all available evidence, the best theory is the one with fewer moving parts.

Having watched thousands of startup pitches, the one thing about good startup ideas is that they're almost always very easy to explain and therefore to understand. If it takes more than a sentence to explain what you're doing, that's almost always a sign that it's way too complicated. Keep working on your message until you boil it down to the essence. Also, the best ideas are usually very different from existing companies, in one crucial way, like Google is a search engine that worked just really well, and none of the other stuff of the portals, or entirely new, like SpaceX. Any startup that is a clone of something else, that already exists, with some new shiny differentiator—like Y, beautiful design, or Z for people that like their eggs sunny side up—usually fails.

Another thing that has nothing to do with the idea itself is the experience and skill set of the founding team. Success has a lot to do with execution, and experienced people know how to execute. If you are an older first entrepreneur leverage your experience and connections; if you are a young first entrepreneur, get the right mentors and pro-actively start learning and experiencing things. Every failure contains valuable lessons, take the time to do a post-mortem with your co-founders so that you learn and don't repeat these mistakes. Likewise, every past success contains parts that are repeatable and if appropriately deployed in your new scenario can lead to a successful outcome.

40 somethings make better entrepreneurs than 20 somethings...

A PERSON WHO IS 40 IS 2.1X MORE LIKELY TO FOUND A SUCCESSFUL STARTUP **THAN A PERSON WHO IS 25**

based on research from MIT and Kellogg on 2.7 million business owners

IT IS NEVER TOO LATE
TO DO A STARTUP!

www.startupbaobook.com

Twenty-somethings do not have a monopoly on great ideas. You should not forego the startup path simply due to your age. Contrary to the perception, the reality is that older entrepreneurs do better than younger ones. According to research on a large number of startups done at Northwestern's Kellog Business school entitled "The Longer You've Been Around, the Better Your Odds." it seems the older the founder, the more likely the startup is to have a successful exit.

Among the 2.7 million founders in the dataset, 41.9 years was the average age of the company's founder at the time of the founding. While it is a big data set, not all of the companies were what we would call startups, though. While the analysis included all kinds of firms, from tech companies to hair salons to restaurants, the bulk of the survey set were high-growth new ventures—the types that can transform the economy—and understanding whether the Silicon Valley myth was true. So when the re-computed of the numbers for only the fastest-growing 0.1 percent (for example, they chose the top 0.1 percent of companies who had the highest revenue or employee growth) the average founder age actually increased to 45.0. "It surprised me," said one of the researchers. "It's even older than I thought." Furthermore when they looked specifically at startups that had successful "exits" (either by getting acquired by another company or going public in an IPO) the average founder age at the time of company founding went up again to 46.7 years.

So the moral of the story is that team, timing, and execution capability are more important than the idea itself. Mythbuster alert: successful startups are not all founded by kids in their 20s! Make sure you and your founding team have the right balance of experience, vision, and passion for taking the idea and making it a market reality. Make sure your product solves a pain point in a market you are invariably very familiar with and that your solution is simple and something you, yourself want to use.

Tao Te Ching 道德经 Verse 76

Men are born soft and supple;

dead they are stiff and hard.

Plants are born tender and pliant;

dead, they are brittle and dry.

Thus whoever is stiff and inflexible

is a disciple of death.

Whoever is soft and yielding

is a disciple of life.

The hard and stiff will be broken.

The soft and supple will prevail.

3

THE PITCH

THE ELEVATOR PITCH: YOUR DAILY DEDICATION TO PRACTICE

If you can't say it in one sentence, your idea (and therefore product/solution) is probably too complicated. The best way to test and refine your idea is to pitch it, regularly. If you don't do the hard work on this part, you WILL miss valuable serendipitous opportunities. All entrepreneurs should work on refining and perfecting their elevator pitches. Make it something you do every day like brushing your teeth. Like a yoga practitioner, practice every day. I do. I also religiously take videos of my public pitches or speeches. After each pitch, I watch it several times by myself and with others who will give me honest feedback. Feedback and constructive criticism are essential! Seek it out, proactively.

You also need a personal elevator pitch in addition to a company elevator pitch because you exist separately from your startup, but as a founder, you are entirely entwined with it. Investors will first and foremost be in investing in you and the founding team, your success. The company and the solution is merely the vehicle for that investment. So create your "personal elevator pitch" that expresses what you have done, excel at doing and plan to do in the future as an entrepreneur.

So, put this book down and set the timer to 30 seconds on your smartphone. Push start! Can you explain what you are capable of doing or creating to a complete stranger in 30 seconds? In your native language? Honestly? Probably not. Can you explain it in a second language? Probably most certainly not. Why is it so hard for people in modern times to explain what they do and are capable of doing? How did things get this way?

> *Ron Conway of SV Angel says, "I am always surprised that more than 25% of the founders we talk to cannot explain in one compelling sentence what the product does. You need to practice your pitch like crazy before you meet investors."*

Successful farmers could always do this throughout history. They can tell you the advantages and disadvantages of their locale, what techniques they have learned to make their yields better, what risks are posed by the weather and the seasons, etc. This compendium of knowledge was written down and became a series of best practices and wise traditions embodied in the Farmer's Almanac. This catalog of extremely useful knowledge became a big part of rural culture. When everyone was a farmer, everyone knew what he or she was good at and how they could contribute to society.

However, the world has changed. With the advent of the Internet, the playing field is leveled. No career is a sure thing anymore. Today, building a career is very similar to the uncertain, rapidly changing conditions in which entrepreneurs start companies. You need to be continually improving your product to meet the needs of an ever-changing market. Moreover, you need to do things you care about in order to retain the passion for what you do.

But what has not changed is this: in the same way all farmers cooperated with others to survive, so must business people today. ALL of the most impactful opportunities in life tend to come from interaction with individuals, not companies. My career got started with a chance meeting with Steve Ballmer of Microsoft at a holiday party. I told him directly I didn't think Microsoft should be satisfied with their business success to date in Japan. In 1 minute, I gave him two examples that showed him how they could do better (and how I could help). Within one week of that conversation, I received an offer letter. Within two weeks I was hired to lead their Japan corporate sales team. I was just 23 years old at the time. That chance meeting and my "elevator pitch" had a huge impact on my life and career vector. It also helped that I was "prepared" with my elevator pitch and fearless (before that I had spent two Summers interning at IBM Japan which was a prime competitor of Microsoft at the time and very successful in Japan).

Your Elevator Pitch:

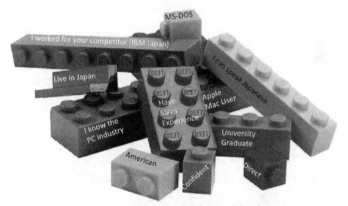

Start with the building blocks

So did I expect to meet Steve Ballmer at that party? No. Was I ready? Yes. The reason I was able to pull off my elevator pitch and have the conversation that changed my life is that I had prepared the "building blocks" of my elevator pitch—long before this chance meeting. Think of it as always keeping the right LEGO pieces in your pocket and being able to pull them out and build something that is relevant and unique for every listener. The graphic above is a representation of the pieces I pulled out of my pocket for the conversation with Steve.

Personal differentiation is the key to your success. Similarly, differentiation is the key to the success of any startup you are involved with. Imagine there are millions of people (or robots?) who can do your job. At 22, I was "differentiated" because I was one of the very few Americans in Japan who spoke the language and knew the computer industry. How will you be better and or different? Ask yourself. Ask people you know. But beware! Sometimes people closest to you give you the worst advice. If your parents are encouraging you to be an accountant or some other "safe" profession, they are not qualified to be advising you.

REED HOFFMAN, SILICON VALLEY INVESTOR, CO-FOUNDER OF PAYPAL AND LINKEDIN SAYS, "YOU REMAKE YOURSELF AS YOU GROW AND AS THE WORLD CHANGES. YOUR IDENTITY DOESN'T GET FOUND. IT EMERGES." ENGAGING WITH AND COLLABORATING WITH PEOPLE IS HOW YOU BECOME SUCCESSFUL IN LIFE. REED GOES ON TO SAY, "NO MATTER HOW BRILLIANT YOUR MIND OR STRATEGY, IF YOU'RE PLAYING A SOLO GAME, YOU'LL ALWAYS LOSE OUT TO A TEAM. THE FASTEST WAY TO CHANGE YOURSELF IS TO HANG OUT WITH PEOPLE WHO ARE ALREADY THE WAY YOU WANT TO BE."

Putting the pieces together in the moment

Means you have to actively think about and practice them

Imagine that every time you talk about your startup you are just using the LEGO pieces you have in your pocket. Taking what Reed Hoffman says to heart, watch a lot of videos that are of people giving pitches on one topic. TED Talks are great for this. Make a practice of watching (repeatedly) people who pitch well. Then video yourself doing your pitch and get constructive criticism from people whose opinion you trust or from those who are better than you at pitching. Focus on making one takeaway per slide. Don't use notes and do not read your slides. Start giving talks yourself. Go to Toastmasters or volunteer to help some organization like Startup Grind that will put you in contact with lots of people who are always speaking in public and making pitches. Sign yourself up for pitch contests. Make doing this part of your new year's resolution. Invite people you know to come out and listen to you so that you get comfortable pitching to friends and family as well as complete strangers. There is only one way to become good at public speaking and pitching: practice lots, do it lots and get lots of feedback. For example, this is so much a part of my routine that besides giving a few talks a month, I will go to pitch contests not to invest but just to see who does the best pitches. Afterward, I go up to each of them and give them unsolicited feedback. I watch how well (or poorly) they take the feedback. The people who pitch the best (or take feedback the best) are the people I seek out to mentor. They are the ones who will have a fighting chance of getting funded. Those who pitch poorly, never solicit feedback and just think they performed well will be the ones who will become disillusioned (and bitter in some cases) when no one invests in them. They will never know that the reason was that they couldn't properly do an elevator pitch.

Following is how I pitch—my process. In the end, a pitch is a high-level summary of the things you know a lot about (yourself, your startup, specific areas of expertise, etc.). For example, this entire book came from a single pitch I prepared for an 8-minute presentation slot to a room packed with over 200 startup entrepreneurs; most of whom were doing their first startup. I wanted to distill down the key things every up-and-coming entrepreneur needs to know—what is essential and what is not. The presentation had eleven slides. This book has eleven chapters. Get the correlation? I could have spoken for an hour or more on any of the slides and in my paid workshops, Udemy course or my Entrepreneurship 201 University Course at the University of International Business and Economics (UIBE) in Beijing, I do speak for an extended period and cover lots of details.

Six Key Points of a Successful Elevator Pitch

1) SMILE AND RELAX
Smile to your counterpart, look them in the eyes and open with a statement, question or handshake that grabs their attention

2) ABOUT YOU
Tell who you are: describe you and your company/career history highlights. Show enthusiasm!

3) WHAT DO YOU OFFER THE LISTENER?
Talk about milestones you have achieved, problems you have solved or contributions you have made. Give details or a clear example if possible.

4) WHAT BENEFITS DO YOU OR YOUR COMPANY/PRODUCT OFFER?
Mention what unique service, product or solutions you or your company offers. What are the advantages of working with you? How are you different from others?

5) HOW DO YOU DO IT? WHAT IS YOUR "SPECIAL SAUCE"?
Give a concrete example or tell a short story, anecdote or analogy, show your uniqueness and paint a verbal picture about how you "do" the thing you do. This can be incorporated into number 4 above to save time

6) CALL TO ACTION
What is the desired next step after your elevator pitch? Do you want a business card, WeChat connection, a referral, follow up meeting, demo, what?

There are two key habits you must form to pitch well.

1) **Be a lifetime learner.** Endeavor to learn something every day, write down what interests you, write articles about things that really interest you and share them with people who are interested in what you are doing or thinking. Whether it is 1, 100, 10,000 or millions, it really doesn't matter. You need to create content and then get real practice sharing it. Don't save the sharing, interacting and learning for the few times you are on the stage. Do it every day in your daily interactions with people.

If you do this you will become more aware of what is going on around you and more people will also become aware of you and what you are interested in. It will also make you a more interesting person and therefore a better speaker.

2) **Do whatever you can to "know" your audience.** I ask questions about the audience to the organizer. I ask questions to the audience at the beginning of my talk. To be an effective speaker, you need to tailor your pitch to the audience

I am a public speaker and am often asked to speak at startup-related events. However, I didn't just wake up one day and was suddenly in demand. It was a process of years. From speaking to my team in Microsoft Japan to speaking at company and customer events as a software industry executive to paid training and University courses, I became a better speaker and became more and more in demand because I worked at it. It took time and lots of practice, and I still work on my technique every day.

One thing I have learned is that most events are poorly organized. I feel it is my duty to help organizers where I can and at the very least do whatever I can do to ensure the event is valuable for the attendees. The way to do that starts with asking the organizer more than a few questions.

I ask a seemingly insane amount of questions to an organizer of an event when they invite me to speak. Based on their answers, I decide to accept or not. You are likely different. You may want to get as much speaking experience as you can. I highly recommend you do so if you are not an established public speaker. Regarding the questions below, it doesn't matter if you are a famous speaker with published books and a successful business to your credit or not. Ask questions! Show that you care about giving the audience a great experience. I usually ask the following questions:

- What is the purpose of the event? Let's hope the organizer can give you a coherent answer. If not, beware!

- What do you want the audience to get out of my presentation? Really. You need to ask this question. If the organizer is clueless on this point, stay away!

- What type of people (background, areas of interest, students, business people, locals/foreign nationals, etc.) do you expect to sign up? I don't take an "all of the above" I actually ask multiple questions about the target audience.

- What is the format? In general, I am not a fan of panel discussions (more often than not, poorly moderated and a complete waste of time) and prefer interactive, focused sessions. Where at all possible I try to mold the format to fit what I want to accomplish with the audience. You would be surprised if you ask for a format change you might well get it. Many organizers are more focused on getting the event done and checking the box than thinking deeply about how to make it most useful for the audience. If you have ideas on the format, etc., you should mention them.

- How many people do you actually expect to attend? The number of attendees makes a big difference in how interactive the session can become. It also can affect your marketing ROI and the organizer's ability to pay you.

- How long do I have in my speaking slot? This is also usually negotiable as well as the order of your slot if there are multiple speakers on the bill.

- Will I be able to use Powerpoint? You need to confirm this (and other relevant logistics) well in advance.

- Will there be time for questions? It is always good to have Q&A if the format allows.

- Who are the other speakers and what will they be talking about? You don't want content overlap you also want the other speakers to be of a certain quality, or you can be painted with the stink that a poorly executed event can bring. While you can't be as choosy when you are just starting to be a public speaker, you also don't want to "that guy will speak anywhere just for a chance to pitch his product." Associate yourself with high-quality events.

- Will you be reviewing the content before the show to ensure quality and applicability to the audience? Can I see what the other presenters will be presenting in advance? Most organizers don't do this but all should because if there are five speakers, the chances are that 3-4 will be so incredibly boring that they put the audience to sleep, or worse yet, checking their phone. All organizers should check the content in advance and give proactive feedback in my opinion. After all, it is their event.

- Is it a paid event or free event? Knowing this will enable you to back of the envelope calculations on what the organizer is making on the event which sets up the next question.

- Is there an honorarium (a fee for the speaker)? You should ask if any speakers are being paid. Even if you are not famous (yet!) and typically earn appearance fees, it is worth asking.

- Are you paying transportation and lodging fees for any of the speakers? If it is going to cost you real money in time, travel and lodging to be there, you should ask this and make it clear you will have to spend your own money if they don't pay or reimburse you for expenses.

- If they are not paying you (and many times if they are), then it is open season to ask the following. How much exposure can I get for my company? Ask if they can put your picture and company logo on the flyer (these days mostly a digital teaser photograph that is used to advertise the event). Also, ask if you can get signage. I often go early and put contact cards on all the chairs or have them put them in the swag bag if they are giving these out. Even if your talk has little to do with your company you can at least promote yourself/your company on the first (intro slide) where you introduce yourself and who you are

- Can you share the email and names (or other contact information) of the attendees so that I may follow up properly? If not, ask them what follow up they will be doing and ask if you can help or participate in any way. In China, a WeChat group is often set up with all the attendees in it. Find out how and when to follow up is going to happen

- Are you recording the event (video, live streaming, audio, podcasting, etc.) the event? How can I get a copy of the output or at least my part? If they aren't recording it, let them know you will be having someone record your portion on video and they need to reserve space up front for your friend/colleague to record it.

- What post-marketing are you going to be doing for the event? Will there be follow up events here or in other locations/cities/countries? If not, ask why not. If so, you may want to ask if you can participate in those activities as well.

Needless to say, a public event where your present, pitch or speak is a great way to get real-world practice, get you and your company's name out there and do some effective grassroots marketing. I have found that people who hear you speak in person are many, many times more likely to use your products or otherwise productively engage with you.

Of course, if no events exist that suit your needs, feel free to create your own. I jumpstarted my mentoring career by doing my private paid events for 10 to 30 people. The contacts I have made and the experiences I have had doing these 2-hour mentoring workshops have proven invaluable to me over my career and form a good part of the foundation for the information you find in the book that you are reading now.

Post-event, talk about the event. Post what you saw, learned and experienced. If you are sharing things with ten people or 1,000 people in a public forum, make sure you take the message out of the room once the event is over so those who didn't make it in person can benefit.

Besides your twitter (or WeChat, Weibo in China), leverage your Facebook, WeChat (if you are in China) and especially your LinkedIn contacts. Linked in is great for this and if you promise a copy of your presentation to those who ask for one in the comments, you can drive up your views and make some excellent connections with people who actually, proactively want your content.

That said, pace yourself. Don't let social media activities, likes, views, forwards and all those things dominate your life. Just build good habits. Do a talk, do some posts before and after. Most of all, keep trying new things and watch what others are doing.

Don't forget what is important in your life: family, friends, and colleagues. Budget time in your schedule where you have nothing in particular scheduled and spend it with people you care about. You need to balance your input and output cycles. Without any time for input of new ideas and experiences, the well that feeds your ability to create output will run dry. And vice-versa. If you never create anything new (I.e., never produce any output), then you will get washed down the river of never-ending inputs from our world that is so overwhelmingly data rich. It took me years of being aware, doing things, starting and running companies, making presentations, writing tidbits down and saving ideas in Evernote to get to the point where I am right now able to tune everything else out and write this book. Fluctuating between intense periods of input and intense periods of output keeps you fresh and growing as a person. Look at your new year's resolutions or your "To Do" lists. They can't be all outputs (e.g., write this book which was on my list at the beginning of the year), at least half of them need to be inputs (e.g., new things you want to learn, like reading, reciting and discussing classic Chinese poetry, this is also on my list this year). You can't do everything, so learning to play guitar didn't make my list this year but maybe it will someday. I couldn't tell you.

Embrace serendipity. Your best elevator pitches will happen in those moments when you are least expecting it. Today, have you met someone new? Drawn or created something with your hands? Walked a different route to a familiar location? Read a new book or article that expands your thinking? Have you asked someone a question instead of just saying, "hello"? Moreover, when you learn something new, do you write it down? If your answer was no to any or all of the above questions, why not start doing these things today? Also, try to find something you can teach or explain to somebody. Teaching someone is the final step in the learning process. That is why it is so sad when I see someone who can not give an elevator pitch. It means you don't know enough about yourself or your company to even explain it briefly and adequately to another human being.

A few words on pitching for VCs. This is also covered in some detail in Chapter 10. When developing content specifically for your investor pitch materials, you should see the process as a competition for the investor's attention. Indeed, in a sense, you are competing against every other opportunity the investor sees across a number market segments. VCs receive thousands of pitches on an annual basis, and each VC will be pitched hundreds of times in a given year. An investor has to determine which requests are worth the initial time investment in with an in-person meeting.

 1. **Idea**    2. **Product**

 3. **Team**    4. **Execution**

Graphic courtesy of YCombinator

The key areas that VCs care about (and therefore you should be able to explain to them) are these four taken from YCombinators "How To Start a Startup" course at Stanford University. They are:

1. Great idea

2. Great product

3. Great team

4. Great execution

For your initial interactions with VCs and investors the key LEGO blocks (in addition to your personal strengths) are as follows:

- What the core idea and what problem you are solving? And how are (in what unique way) are you solving it?

- What is your product value proposition? Why would someone pay for your product and who would pay (target customer segment). B-to-B versus B-to-C solutions will have slightly different approaches, but the key is to make the example extremely straightforward.

- The Team. Why you? What makes you and your founding team the right people to execute on this idea (versus someone else)?

- Execution. Why now? What makes you feel the timing is right (not too early, not too late)? How quickly can you scale the business, grow the revenue? What are the key factors involved?

None of these answers are simple and how clearly and quickly you answer will say a lot about you as an entrepreneur. At the end of the day, the VC is investing in you and your founding team. The best way to make a great impression is to have your elevator pitch so well-honed you can do it anytime, anywhere without thinking about it. Like a well-trained athlete uses his/her well-trained muscle memory.

Muscle memory is "the ability to repeat a specific muscular movement with improved efficiency and accuracy that is acquired through practice and repetition." Merriam - Webster Dictionary

---

Don't practice until you get it right. Practice your pitch until you can't get it wrong.

Tao Te Ching 道德经 Verse 66

All streams flow to the sea because it is lower than they are.

Humility gives it its power.

If you want to govern the people, you must place yourself below them.

If you want to lead the people, you must learn how to follow them.

The Master is above the people, and no one feels oppressed.

He goes ahead of the people, and no one feels manipulated.

The whole world is grateful to him.

Because he competes with no one, no one can compete with him.

4

THE CO-FOUNDERS

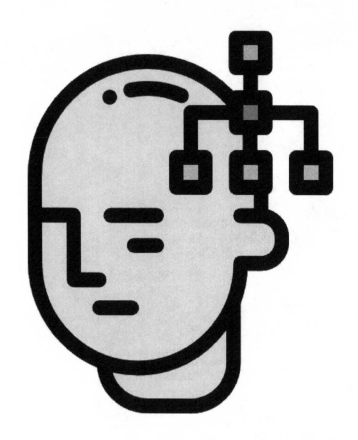

CHOOSING CO-FOUNDER(S): THE MOST IMPORTANT DECISION

Assembling the right founding team is without a doubt the most crucial decision would-be entrepreneurs face. It impacts almost everything you do in the beginning. You need to spend the time, and effort to get this right! If you get it wrong, you can get a bunch of other things right, and you'll still likely fail. In China and around the world I do workshops specifically focused on this particular topic. It is just that important. The best idea in the world and the best elevator pitch cannot be turned into a winning product and company without a good, balanced founding team.

Out of the top 20 reasons startups fail, most have a component that is related to founder issues. Don't do a startup by yourself. If you are trying to do a startup by yourself, it tells investors that you can't convince anyone to join you, or your idea is terrible, or both. The only one person startups are artists or consultants.

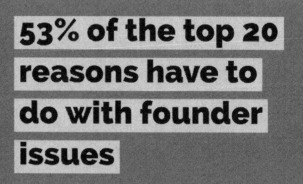

53% of the top 20 reasons have to do with founder issues

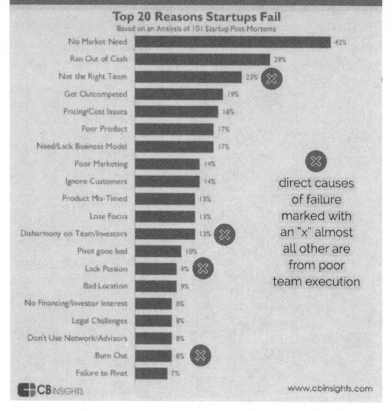

Top 20 Reasons Startups Fail
Based on an Analysis of 101 Startup Post-Mortems

Reason	%
No Market Need	42%
Ran Out of Cash	29%
Not the Right Team	23%
Get Outcompeted	19%
Pricing/Cost Issues	18%
Poor Product	17%
Need/Lack Business Model	17%
Poor Marketing	14%
Ignore Customers	14%
Product Mis-Timed	13%
Lose Focus	13%
Disharmony on Team/Investors	13%
Pivot gone bad	10%
Lack Passion	9%
Bad Location	9%
No Financing/Investor Interest	8%
Legal Challenges	8%
Don't Use Network/Advisors	8%
Burn Out	8%
Failure to Pivot	7%

direct causes of failure marked with an "x" almost all other are from poor team execution

CBINSIGHTS

www.cbinsights.com

Following are the most important things to consider about your co-founder. In this section, I will use the words co-founder and co-founders interchangeably. Also, the reason I will use the word co-founder is that I have "Golden Rule" in this regard. Most experienced startup entrepreneurs and investors agree to the following:

- One founder is not enough

- Two is great

- Three can be OK given the nature of the startup and assuming a clear separation of duties

- Four or more is asking for trouble (except for certain consultancy startups)

When it comes to deciding to invest or not, the biggest factor for VCs is whether they believe the founding team can make it happen or not. So get your founding team right! Another thing VCs look at is how well you know each other and how long you have worked together previously. The classic examples all come to mind here.

Steve Jobs and Steve Wozniak worked knew each other since their teenage years. Their first collaboration was not the Apple Computer that made them famous. In fact, they worked together on a phone hacking device and were bonafide "phone phreaks" before forming Apple. A phone phreak is someone who breaks into the telephone network illegally, usually for the making free long-distance phone calls or to tap phone lines. Phone phreaking began in the late 1950s and was at was at its peak in the late 1960s and early 1970s. The term first referred to groups who had reverse engineered the system of tones used to route long-distance calls. Later, people like Wozniak and Jobs created and marketed single purpose "blue boxes." These boxes emulated the in-band signaling tones used by the telephone exchanges.

Playing these tones through a speaker connected to the telephone handset's microphone tricked the automatic exchanges into thinking that they were receiving legitimate signaling information. They allegedly made a total of $6,000 from selling their blue boxes. Later, when the police nearly caught Wozniak and Jobs, the two stopped making the boxes and gave up their innocent, yet quasi-criminal activities and moved on to building circuit boards. According to Jobs, Apple would not have been possible had it not been for the experiments that Wozniak and he did designing, perfecting and building the blue boxes.

Their skill sets and roles were different, and they had already established a successful collaborative working relationship before forming Apple Computer. The same goes for Bill Gates and Paul Allen. They learned computers together at Seattle's Lakeside School when they were 12 and 14 years old respectively and formed a company together before Microsoft called "Traf-o-Data." As members of the Lakeside Programmers Group in the 1970s, they got free computer time on various computers in exchange for writing code. Gates and Allen thought they could process the traffic data quicker than the local companies. Utilizing classmates to manually read the hole-patterns in the paper tape and transcribe the data onto computer cards, Gates then used a computer at the University of Washington to produce the traffic flow charts they were in business to sell. Coincidentally urban planning issues were also a topic of discussion between Stanford University graduate students Larry Page and Sergey Brin. They met on campus in the Summer of 1995. According to others who knew them, they became embroiled in an argument at their first meeting, mainly about alternate approaches to urban planning. They both have said they recall thinking of one another as "obnoxious." Stanford collaborated on several projects including what became Google. The three founders of Airbnb also were friends, and all lived together. Because two of them didn't have jobs and they couldn't pay the rent, they bought a few airbeds and quickly put up a site called "Air Bed and Breakfast." The idea was to offer visitors a place to sleep and breakfast in the morning. They charged $80 each a night. The idea succeeded and the first Airbnb guests were born: a 30-year-old Indian man, a 35-year-old woman from Boston and a 45-year-old father of four from Utah sleeping on their floor.

SUCCESS TIMELINE AIRBNB

October 2007 — Idea Creation

August 2008 — Launched AirBedandBreakfast.com

August to November 2008 — Sold cereal boxes and earned $30000

January 2009 — Accepted into Y Combinator. Received $20000 as funding.

March 2009 — Website becomes airbnb.com

November 2010 — Received funding of $7.2 Million

February 2011 — Reached 1 millionth booking mark

July 2011 — Received funding of $112 Million

January 2012 — Reaches 5 Millionth booking mark

June 2012 — Reaches 10 millionth booking mark

August 2014 — Received funding of $475 Million

October 2014 — A law named Airbnb Law was made in San Francisco

June 2015 — Received funding of $1.5 Billion

November 2015 — Private Equity Funding of $100M

December 2015 — Received funding of $1.5 Billion

March 2017 — Received funding of $447.8M

September 2018 — Received funding of $555.5M

Contrast these stories with the founders of Facebook. No one remembers the other co-founders of Facebook. Nor should they, because Facebook didn't need five co-founders. Only Mark Zuckerberg of the original five still works there today. Zuckerberg's sheer force of will got Facebook through the fallout and separation of the four other founders. As companies and founding stories go, it is an outlier. Most startups do not survive the departure of most of the founding team, nor do most successful startups have five founders.

Facebook, Inc. › Founders

| Mark Zuckerberg | Dustin Moskovitz | Eduardo Saverin | Andrew McCollum | Chris Hughes |

As I mentor startups, I notice two cases that stand out among first-time founders. The first is a founder that can not find a co-founder and is considering starting the company by themselves. The other is more like the Facebook dynamic described above where the person leading the startup process just can't say no, and basically, everyone who to-date has been even peripherally involved in the startup becomes a co-founder. Early employees' and co-founder's commitment levels to the startup are profoundly different, and the two should never be confused.

Most people who start companies already have a day job. Everyone who is a founder should have a timeline and a clear set of criteria for when and how they will be joining full time soon. All compensation; stock, salary or otherwise should be tied to the date the co-founder joins full time—no exceptions. I suggest every cofounder take "The Founder Test."

The Founder Test		Yes	Maybe	No
1) Agreement	Do the other founders think of you as a founder, someone absolutely essential to the success of the startup?			
2) Relationships	Do you have a pre-existing working relationship with at least one of the other founders?			
3) Part/Full Time	Do you have a plan to join the startup full-time very soon?			
4) Sacrifice	Are you prepared to forgo other life opportunities in order to achieve the goals of the startup?			
5) Finances	Do you expect or need to be paid by the startup from the beginning?			
6) Skills	Do your skills and experience set balance those of your co-founders (i.e. are you good at different things)?			

Having each potential co-founder take this test forces the discussions that need to happen. Any "No's" or "Maybe's" are potential red flags and what is behind them must be probed and revealed to all. Providing a starting point for the goal setting when you are building the Minimum Viable Product (MVP) and the equity ownership discussions that need to happen sooner rather than later. More often than not, you will be surprised at some of the answers of your co-founders. You may discover they are just doing this between jobs or as a way to learn new skills (see questions 3-4 above). You also may have assumed wrongly about their willingness to forego pay (question 5). Their individual money management habits will be (good or bad) to the startup. Each co-founder's financial situation always comes up as a topic of discussion when doing a startup. Those that contribute money and time will have issues eventually with those who only contribute time. These things all need to be discussed and documented (we will explain the how this should be recorded later in the chapter)

So how do you choose the right co-founder? This is, without a doubt, the most critical decision of your startup and more than likely the next several years of your life. The only thing it is comparable to in "real life" is choosing your marriage partner. So be serious about the decision and go into the process with your eyes and ears wide open.

Here are some key considerations for you:

1) Different Skill Set. Make sure your co-founders are good at doing things you aren't good at doing. While your goals and passion around the startup should be wholly aligned, your operational skill sets and expertise should be completely different. If you are a sales and marketing rainmaker, then your co-founder should be a technical wizard. Industry experience is helpful but not necessary as if you are doing a real startup (not a scale up or small business, see Chapter 1) then most of what you will be doing will be very new and likely be stuff that has never been done before.

2) Working History Together. It is always preferable to have a history of working together. If you have worked on a project together in the same company or done a startup before then, you already have a strong sense of what your potential co-founder is capable of and what kind of work ethic he/she has. When I say history, I don't mean friends or family members as those are the people you should definitely not be doing your startup with. Also the more workplace ups and downs you have experienced together, the better. You never really know a person until problems arise. If you have already walked through fire together then the better equipped you will be to get through the rigors of the startup odyssey.

3) Balanced Temperments and Different Personalities.
If you are an introvert, it is better to have a co-founder that is more outgoing. If you are great at vision but miss details make sure you have a partner that will not miss things. If you are a hot-headed, opinionated person, it is essential to ensure your co-founders can balance you by bringing calm and clarity to meetings. Your co-founders need to be able to call you out when you may have gone too far, or not considered all the critical data. Everyone can learn to do things, but if you end up being responsible for the things you are comfortable with and do well, you will be more efficient as a team. Bill Gates knew enough about coding to be slightly dangerous, but they certainly did not write any of the code on which Microsoft built its fortune. Steve Ballmer was good at rallying teams to complete specific goals, but he faltered as CEO where a different style was required. The more diverse, in personality your startup founding team is, the more likely your customers and investors will find one or more of you they like.

4) Similar Work Habits. Your co-founders need to be OK with being called at any time night and day if that is your startup's vibe. If one of you unplugs on the weekends and the other two founders are non-stop every day of the week then it will become an issue. If one founder is late for everything and the other(s) are always on time, this will stress the relationships and endanger the startup's viability. Be on the same wavelength about how and when you work.

5) Self-Motivated and Action-Oriented. In almost every startup team with more than two founders, this issue is widely prevalent and more often than not becomes an issue. Some people are oriented to being told what to do and not thinking or acting independently. A person like this has no business being a startup co-founder. Employee perhaps, but co-founder, absolutely not! Also, this approach completely embraces the "if you are not a part of the solution, you are part of the problem" philosophy. If something is not working or a process is broken, suggest (or better yet create) a solution and fix it.

6) Dedication to Honest Over-Communication. In a startup, assumptions kill. You can not assume anything. Anything. So there is no excuse for not over-communicating. Don't expect your co-founder(s) know what you are doing or what you found out today. Tell them. Decide how you communicate. At yoli we run the entire company in WeChat (China-specific chat-based super app), and we never use email. We only have one scheduled meeting per week for 1 hour (also done on WeChat), and we never miss it or change it. Anything individually we learn, find out, do, etc., is communicated immediately in WeChat. And because WeChat is like a river, when you throw a message in a bottle into the river it isn't long before it flows downstream. Therefore anything that becomes a company learning or impacts planning, processes, etc., is documented in Evernote. Everything is shared, communicated real-time, and the critical stuff is documented. This removes the need for frequent meetings and the honesty and the dedication to "over-communication" ensures that the business of the company is entirely transparent and nothing anyone needs to know is withheld or left un-communicated. This "over-communication" works for my team at yoli. You need to create your own culture of communication in your startup.

7) Emotional Balance. In a startup there are lots of great high-fiving days, days like you feel on top of the world. However, the highs are also balanced with some measure of monotony, and bad days, frustrating moments, bad deals that fall through for no apparent reason, failed sales and marketing efforts, activities that waste money you don't have to spend, awesome features that end up sucking when implemented, etc. On those days your friendship will get you through. A well-timed joke or some time talking about something other than your startup can work wonders. I co-founded my first two companies with the same guy. I was the outgoing, flamboyant one and my highs were higher, and lows were lower than my co-founder. He was always unfazed by setbacks and could always articulate what the silver lining was for us when the dark clouds gathered. That is what you need in a co-founder. I am sure he benefitted from my boundless (sometimes unrealistically so) optimism, but he was the one you wanted with a hand on the rudder in the tough times.

8) No False Pretenses. Ego, fear, and insecurities can kill a relationship. The best startup co-founders create "fear-free" environment just like you had with your best friends in high school. You can say and do anything and be yourself without worrying about someone taking something you say the wrong way. The best co-founders themselves (and eventually you) well and are comfortable in their own skins. Everyone should check his or her egos at the door and be extremely clear about their respective roles and responsibilities.

9) Compatibility and Respect. You have to like AND respect your co-founders. It seems obvious, but it apparently isn't given the number of dysfunctional startup founding teams I have seen. You're going to spend a lot of time with each other, probably more than you do with your girlfriend, spouse, children or family. It is crucial you like each other as people. Enough said.

10) Alignment on the Core Vision. Your co-founder(s) and you should have a shared vision. And it should sound 99% the same when each of you articulates it. Yes, say it to each other, practice pitching each other (see Chapter 3 on the Elevator Pitch). This is something you need to re-affirm and double-check frequently. With each new product iteration or the inevitable strategy pivots (both minor or massive) you need to sit down and pitch the new vision to each other. You need to look for the commitment (or lack of) in the eyes and body language of your co-founders when they pitch you. Just like the story, you tell when someone asks you "how did you meet your wife?" your versions of the story should be in alignment. If not, the fissures and rifts in the foundation will only become larger with each passing day.

11) Core Motivation. At the end of the day getting to know the deep-rooted motivation of your co-founders is incredibly important. While all statistics show the most likely way for anyone to become wealthy is own part of a company, my experience tells me that the people who focus on money first and foremost are not likely to succeed. This is one of the reasons for the title of this book: The Tao of Startups. In Daoist philosophy, anything you try for too hard or too directly will almost always not come to pass or if it does will lead you to destruction. The man who works too hard to attract the perfect woman. The chef who focuses too hard to get that ever-elusive Michelin four-star rating for his restaurant. Trying too hard to do something upsets the natural equilibrium of nature.

If that was too much information to digest, have a look at YCombinator's (YC) key points from this "Cliff Notes" version I put together.

According to YC, the best co-founders have the following traits:

- Ability to clearly articulate vision. And have the same shared vision

- Very determined (people that bend the world around their will) and not easily discouraged

- "Get" the mission. They feel that what they are doing is very important and positively impacts the world or their customers

- Raw Intelligence

- Ability to work quickly, decide quickly. Problem-solving

Biggest co-founder issues according to YC

- Too many co-founders. Prefer 2 or 3 co-founders. All YC single founders funded found a co-founder afterward. The psychological toll of being a solo founder is high. But it is worse to have a bad co-founder. Start working in solo mode but never stop looking for a co-founder. More than three founders. Someone typically leaves early.

- Founders that want to build a different company or both want the same role in the company.

- Startups that hire too many people too fast. Airbnb didn't hire for the first nine months. Stripe and Dropbox were the same.

While I agree with YC's points above, as we all know from university just sopping up the key points from a sage is no substitute for actually experiencing something. Even YC's Sam Altman says that these core "rules of thumb" get you only 30% of the way there. Every startup is unique and 70% of it "can't be taught." It must be experienced. That said I strongly believe that understanding each co-founder's core motivation is key to the long-term success of the team. That's why I am going to take you into some of the motivational constructs behind founder selection that I have found extremely useful in my own entrepreneurial career.

There is one key thing that you need to learn if you are ever going to lead an organization effectively and that is the conflux of factors that drive the motivation of human beings. Unless you endeavor to understand this and become able to create and manage an environment where people are incredibly motivated you couldn't build a successful company if Steve Jobs built it for you and handed you the keys to the kingdom. The first concept you need to understand is Maslow's hierarchy of needs. Proposed by Abraham Maslow in his 1943 paper "A Theory of Human Motivation" in Psychological Review, it is most often represented with a five-tier model of human needs.

Needs lower down in the hierarchy must be satisfied before individuals can begin to address needs higher up. From the bottom of the hierarchy upwards, the needs are physiological, safety, love and belonging, esteem and self-actualization.

Maslow's Hierarchy of Needs

Maslow's Theory is powerful in a broad sense. But to understand how human motivation works in companies and other such organizations I need to introduce you to a researcher named Frederick Herzberg who took what he learned from all the great behavioral researchers such as Pavlov, Maslow, and countless others and applied it to what motivates white collar workers.

In the 1950s Herzberg studied 200 engineers and accountants in the US. He asked them a few simple questions and came up with what is one of the most widely-accepted theories on job satisfaction called "Two Factor Theory."

Herzberg's Two Factor Theory breaks job satisfaction into two factors:

- Hygiene factors such as working conditions, quality of supervision, salary, safety, and company policies.

- Motivation factors such as achievement, recognition, responsibility, the work itself, personal growth, and advancement.

Net/net personal satisfaction has a lot more to do with Motivation factors than Hygiene factors for the vast majority of people. In the modern world, the motivators are much more important than actual pay. Now perhaps you are starting to see it. Startups are by nature Low Hygiene and High Motivation environments. A startup team by definition should be extremely sensitive to motivational factors and pretty much numb to hygiene factors.

A startup is most definitely a Low Hygiene (low salary, long hours, lack of hierarchy and supervision) and High Motivation (possibility for personal growth, recognition, achievement and satisfying work). That is why startups resemble cults.

One definition of "cult" in the Merriam-Webster dictionary: *"a great devotion to a person, idea, object, movement, or work."*

Anyone who has been in a startup (or married to someone in a startup) has a visceral understanding of this definition of cult.

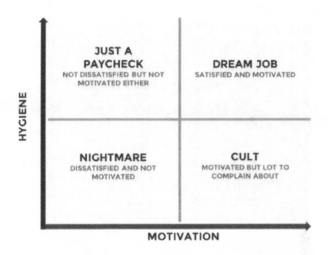

Especially with regard to salary, so many traditional managers think of motivation differently and are just so completely wrong. At the end of the day as a manager or a company, all you can aspire to is that employees will not be mad at each other and the company because of compensation. That is a core truth about all the "hygiene factors." A sudden improvement in hygiene factors at work will not result in immediately measurable job satisfaction or motivation. At best, you won't hate your job anymore. Think about it. The opposite of job dissatisfaction isn't job satisfaction, but instead an absence of job dissatisfaction. These aren't the same thing at all.

IT IS ESSENTIAL TO ADDRESS HYGIENE FACTORS SUCH AS A SAFE AND COMFORTABLE WORKING ENVIRONMENT, RELATIONSHIP WITH MANAGERS AND COLLEAGUES, ENOUGH MONEY TO LOOK AFTER YOUR FAMILY—IF YOU DON'T HAVE THESE THINGS, YOU'LL EXPERIENCE DISSATISFACTION WITH YOUR WORK. BUT THESE ALONE WON'T DO ANYTHING TO MAKE YOU LOVE YOUR JOB—THEY WILL JUST STOP YOU FROM HATING IT. - CLAYTON CHRISTENSEN, "HOW WILL YOU MEASURE YOUR LIFE"

The things that will truly, deeply satisfy us, and cause us to love our jobs are the motivators defined by Herzberg's research. These include challenging work, recognition, responsibility, and personal growth. Feelings that you are making a meaningful contribution to work arise from intrinsic conditions of the work itself. Generations of management thought, best practices and process have been predicated on exactly the wrong things. External "hygiene" factors designed to stimulate the worker. Motivation, it turns out, is about what's inside of you, and inside of your work.

The theory of motivation suggests you need to ask yourself a different set of questions than most of us are used to asking. Is this work meaningful to me? Is this job going to give me a chance to develop? Am I going to learn new things? Will I have an opportunity for recognition and achievement? Am I going to be given responsibility? These are the things that will truly motivate you. Once you get this right, the more measurable aspects of your job will fade in importance.

Many other researchers have taken Herzberg's original findings and not only validated them but have significantly expanded them. Recent behavioral research indicates we're happiest when we're learning new skills or challenging old ones. Two University of Columbia researchers suggesting that workers would be glad to forgo as much as a 20% raise if it meant a job with more variety or one that required more skill. This research suggests that we are willing to be paid less for work that's interesting, fun, and teaches us new skills.

Maslow meets Herzberg in the startup world. Basically, I will explain how the entire concept of a startup takes everything you know or have learned in an established company and turns it upside down. The takeaway is that you and your co-founder(s) needs to be a non-typical person(s) for your startup to be successful.

And it goes beyond yourself and your co-founders. All early employees—and if you get your company culture right, all employees—should be evaluated according to this combination of Maslow/Herzberg lense. Herzberg's research is a valuable lesson that I have learned and re-learned throughout my startup career. I can't tell you how many of the startup co-founders, including my own, have asked me, "how do we hire good people if we don't have any money?". The answer is that the people you need—those will the best fit—will not be motivated by money. You need to be talking to them in the Maslow/Herzberg framework. If the fit is right, they will come to work with you regardless of the money.

Let me break it down for you. It is clear from Maslow that a co-founder must be well clear of the basic psychological and needs for safety. Assuming your co-founder is okay with eating ramen and sleeping on the couch and working with no guarantee of income, then it is important to explore what their needs are. If the co-founder is mainly a part of the team due to social or needs for status or esteem, then there is some need for concern as a change in group dynamics or fear of failure could lead to severe dissatisfaction. Honestly, I encourage anyone considering a co-founder to dig deep enough with questions and observation to get a feel if your potential co-founder has a chance of reaching the top of the hierarchy, self-actualization via his/her role in the startup.

As a startup co-founder, you will find yourself doing many tasks. Some you enjoy doing, many you don't. Some you find fulfilling, some you don't. Some that you excel at, but many that you aren't able to execute as well as someone who is better trained or has more experience than you.

So motivation becomes an issue on a daily basis as Steve Jobs famously said at the 2005 Stanford Commencement Address. A startup founder needs to be properly oriented in Maslow's hierarchy so that he/she can walk out the door with a kick in their step knowing they are learning, growing and doing precisely what they want to be doing.

For the past 33 years, I have looked in the mirror every morning and asked myself: 'If today were the last day of my life, would I want to do what I am about to do today?' And whenever the answer has been 'No' for too many days in a row, I know I need to change something.

Steve Jobs

Stated another way, motivation factors are about the actual job itself. For example, just how exciting the work is and how much opportunity there is for added responsibility, recognition and promotion. Hygiene factors are those which 'surround the job' rather than the job itself. For example, a worker will only show up to work if a business has provided for a decent level of pay and safe working conditions, but these factors will not make he/she work harder at his job once there.

So the key summary for the Herzberg Two-Factor Theory as it applies to startups:

1. Workers are driven to work harder by motivators, e.g., more responsibility, more interesting work, learning opportunities, career advancement opportunities, etc.

2. Workers can become de-motivated and disengage if key hygiene factors are not met, e.g., pay, working conditions, relationships with supervisors and colleagues, etc.

These are the areas you need to understand about your potential co-founders. How much will hygiene factors potentially demotivate them and which particular motivators mean most to them. This should be discussed amongst yourselves and articulated clearly. I suggest writing them down. This will drive transparency and keep people honest.

Startup vs. Corporate jobs

Some (actually, most) people—including your potential co-founder—are happier and better off working for someone else. They should not be doing a startup. Moreover, you should not be trying to co-found a company with them. For example, ask someone who works at a big tech company what's great about their job. If they reply "cool offices, free food, and massages, great benefits" or something else along those lines, then they are telling you subconsciously that they aren't doing it for the work itself but mostly for Hygiene Factors. If these truly are the "best" parts of their job then why do none of them have anything to do with the job itself? This type of response, this type of person is a red flag for a startup. Bringing on someone like this is like putting a lump of Kryptonite in Superman's pocket. It is going to sap the life out of him. These people will kill your startup as co-founders before you even get started. Go find a fellow cult member instead!

As stated earlier, Herzberg's Two Factor Theory explains this. Job satisfaction comes from motivators: challenging work, recognition for achievement, responsibility, opportunity to do meaningful work, involvement in decision making, the ability to make an incredible impact on society. These things resonate with entrepreneurs. As a founder, you have:

- Challenging work. A startup is creating something that hasn't existed before. To do this, you will be challenging the status quo and be highly challenged in return. Being a founder is a continuous learning curve.

- Recognition for your achievement. You won't have the annual review and promotion possibilities that a corporate job has, but you will have a deep sense of fulfillment from what you are achieving as a founder.

- Responsibility. You make the tough calls. You decide. In the end, you are responsible for your team, your investors and your customers.

- A sense of meaning. You have the opportunity to do something meaningful and work on things that you care about.

- Ability to make decisions. You are the primary decision maker and are deciding what your company should do on a micro and macro level.

- A sense of importance to an organization. As the founder, you are central and absolutely crucial to the organization and how it functions.

Founding a startup isn't for everybody. Some people will read that list and shiver with fear at how hard it sounds. But if you read it and honestly can't imagine spending your life working where none of those things apply, then what are you waiting for?

Then there is also the role of the CEO. Which of the co-founders will take that on? This is the most crucial role in the startup, and someone needs to do it. I haven't heard of any successful startups where this role was shared on a permanent basis. Every company needs one person who has the final say on things. Once you have assembled the co-founding team, the next key decision is who will be the CEO.

As the 33rd president of the United States of America, Harry Truman was fond of saying, "The buck stops here!" He also would explain what the saying meant as follows, "The President--whoever he is--has to decide. He can't pass the buck to anybody. No one else can do the deciding for him. That's his job."

There are lots of definitions and even more misconceptions about the role of the CEO in a startup. I personally find this definition by Sam Altman, president of YCombinator one of the best I have come across so I will share it with you here:

The role of the CEO is basically to figure out and decide what the company should do and then make sure it does that. There are a few other things that only the CEO can do, or that the CEO at least has to be heavily involved in, like recruiting and evangelizing the company to new hires, large customers, investors, whatever. But the only universal job description of CEO is making sure the company wins. And so deciding what the company is going to do and making sure the company gets that done—that's the most critical part of the job. The hard part is that most people want to just do the first part, which is figuring out what the company should do. In practice, time-wise, I think the job is 5% that and 95% making sure that it happens. And the annoying thing to many CEOs is that the way you make it happen is incredibly repetitive. It's a lot of the same conversation again and again with employees or press or customers. You have to relentlessly say, "This is what we're doing, this is why, and this is how we're going to do it." And that part—the communication and the evangelizing of the company vision and goals—is time-wise by far the biggest part of the job.

After taking the founders test and having the hard discussions about each other's personal needs (Maslow) and motivations (Herzberg), I always share the founder of Equire.com Paul DeJoe's quora.com answer to the question "What Does It Feel Like To Be The CEO Of A Startup?" It is reproduced in full below.

Very tough to sleep most nights of the week. Weekends don't mean anything to you anymore. Closing a round of financing is not a relief. What it actually means is that now there are many more people depending on you to turn their investment into 20 times what they gave you.

It's very difficult to "turn it off." But at the same time, television, movies, and vacations become so boring to you when your company's future might be sitting in your inbox or in the results of a new A/B test you decide to run.

You feel guilty when you're doing something you like doing outside of the company. Only through years of wrestling with this internal fight do you recognize how the word "balance" is an art that is just as important as any other skill set you could ever hope to have. . . .

You start to respect the duck. Paddle like hell under the water and be smooth and calm on top where everyone can see you. You learn the hard way that if you lose your cool, you lose. You always ask yourself if I am changing the world in a good way? Are people's lives better for having known me?

You start to see that the word "entrepreneur" is a personality. It's difficult to talk to your friends that are not risking the same things you are because they are content with not pushing themselves or putting it all out there in public with the likelihood of failure staring at you everyday (sic). You start to turn a lot of your conversations with relatives into how they might exploit opportunities for profit. Those close to you will view your focus as something completely different because they don't understand. You don't blame them. They can't know if they haven't done it themselves. It's why you will gravitate toward other entrepreneurs. You will find reward in helping other entrepreneurs.

You have to be willing to sleep in your car and laugh about it. You have to be able to laugh at many things because when you think of the worse (sic) things in the world that could happen to your company, they will happen. Imagine working for something for two years and then have (sic) to throw it out entirely because you see in one day that it's wrong. You realize that if your team is having fun and can always laugh that you won't die, and in fact, the opposite will happen: You will learn to love the journey and look forward to what you do everyday (sic) even at the lowest times. You'll hear not to get too low when things are bad and not to get too high when things are good, and you'll even give that advice. But you'll never take it because being in the middle all the time isn't exciting and an even keel is never worth missing out on something worth celebrating. You'll become addicted to finding the hardest challenges because there's a direct relationship between how difficult something is and the euphoria of a feeling when you do the impossible.

You realize that it was much more fun when you didn't (sic) have money, and that money might be the worst thing you could have as a personal goal. If you're lucky enough to genuinely feel this way, it is a surreal feeling that is the closest thing to peace because you realize it's the challenges and the work that you love. Your currencies are freedom, autonomy, responsibility, and recognition. Those happen to be the same currencies of the people you want around you. You feel like a parent to your customers in that they will never realize how much you love them and it is they who validate you are not crazy. You want to hug every one of them. They mean the world to you. You learn the most about yourself more than any other vocation as an entrepreneur. You learn what you do when you get punched in the face many many times. You learn what you do when no one is looking and when no one would find out. You learn that you are bad at many things, lucky if you're good at a handful of things and the only thing you can ever be great at is being yourself which is why you can never compromise it.

You become incredibly grateful for the times that things were going as bad as they possibly could. Most people won't get to see this in any other calling. When things are really bad, there are people that come running to help and don't think twice about it. I will forever be in their debt I, and you can never repay them nor would they want or expect to be repaid.

You begin to realize that in life, the luckiest people in the world only get one shot at being a part of something great. Knowing this helps you make sense of your commitment.

Of all the things said though, it is an amazing thing to go through--every day is different and so exciting. Even when it's bad, it's exciting. Knowing that your decisions will not only affect you but many others is a weight that I would rather have any day than the weight of not controlling my future. That's why I could not do anything else.

Founding a startup isn't for everybody. Some people will read this chapter and Paul DeJoe's post and shiver with fear at how hard it sounds. But if you read it and honestly can't imagine spending your life working somewhere where none of those things apply, then what are you waiting for?

Tao Te Ching 道德经 Verse 57

To rule the state, have a known plan

To win a battle, have an unknown plan

To gain the universe, have no plan at all

Let the universe itself reveal to you its splendor

How do I know this should be so?

Because of this —

The more restrictions, the more poverty

The more weapons, the more fear in the land

The more cleverness, the more strange events

The more laws, the more lawbreakers

Thus as the Sages say,

Act with a pure heart and the people will be

transformed

Love your own life and the people will be uplifted

Give without conditions and the people will prosper

Want nothing and the people will find everything

5

THE MVP

MVP: FOCUS ON WHAT IS IMPORTANT FIRST

This is by far the longest chapter in this book, and it is packed full of actionable information and thought-provoking exercises as well as solid techniques you can use immediately. Since the MVP process is the point where everything in a startup goes from ideas, "what could be" dreams, and plans to the "WTF" and invigorating often brutal reality of competition and of taking hard-earned money from people for this thing you and your cofounders created. This chapter is about the time in your startup life where the rubber meets the road. So buckle up, and let's get going!

Elon Musk famously said he never created a business plan. I don't think you need to either. However, you need to think seriously about your "business model." You need to explain it to investors as it evolves. However, I find most first time entrepreneurs are intimidated by this. So let's discuss and define what a business model is.

A business model is a plan of action for profitably operating the business in a specific marketplace. Your business model will be inextricably aligned with your unique value proposition. So it follows that the business model for a retail shop is significantly different from the business model for an online business, for example.

The Business Model Canvas (BMC) is a tool used to quickly and easily define and communicate a business idea or concept. It is a convenient one-page document which displays the fundamental elements of a business or product, in a format that is easily viewed and compared. The right side of the BMC focuses on the customer (external), while, the left side focuses on the business (internal).

Above is the Airbnb Business Model Canvas. In many of my mentoring sessions when I put this BMC up on the screen with no labels, it usually only takes about a minute or so for keen students to realize that this is indeed Airbnb's BMC.

That is the power of the BMC. You can capture a business' entire business model on one page. Therefore I highly suggest you use this template to flesh out your business model. For more information and samples of business models that may be similar to your startup's, take a look at the Business Model Gallery which boasts the "World's Largest Business Model Database"

In the early days as you are building your MVP it makes sense to put the bulk of your focus on fleshing out what I call the "inverted T", as it looks like an upside down letter "T" when you look at these three areas on a standard "Business Model Canvas" The three core pillars of the business model, are the value proposition, revenue streams and costs associated with those revenue streams.

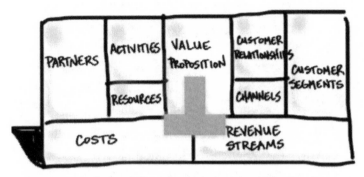

Note the "**inverted T**". Get those right first! Then fill out the others.

The first thing you must tell anyone considering investing in your business is the value proposition. A value proposition is defined as a concise statement of a company's offering (i.e., products and services) that is of value to potential customers or clients, stated in a way that differentiates the company from its competitors. The revenue streams are the way you monetize the value proposition (e.g. how and how much you get paid, for what) and the costs should be understood in two ways: 1) the intrinsic cost per transaction and 2) the overall costs per item or transaction that includes your infrastructure, rent, salaries, cost of goods, etc.

The business model will evolve with the company and therefore over time should incorporate the costs of building, maintaining and supporting the product/service; marketing strategy and spend; partnering costs, and future projections of revenues and expenses. One of the most common mistakes made by startup founders is a failure to make projections of all expenses necessary to fund the business to the point of profitability, i.e., the point in time when revenues exceed expenses. That is why the above matrix is one you should always keep in your mind.

Furthermore, a business model should include any potential plans for partnering with other existing businesses. An example of this would be a mobile phone game publisher that plans to build a game based on another company's characters or stories. As the company I co-founded, Yodo1 did with Hasbro's Transformers Earth Wars.

Below is an example of the template I use in my mentoring workshops with the "Inverted T" highlighted. Whether you write this on a whiteboard or on paper, the founding team should do the exercise, record it and refer to it (and update it) as the business model evolves.

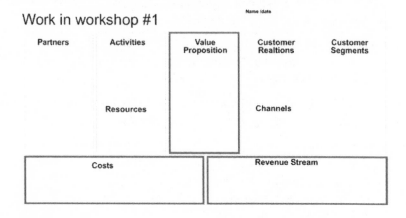

For speaking with investors, you often need to understand the variety of business models that exist and be able to explain what type of business model your company uses. Some of the more common business model types are:

Manufacturer

A manufacturer creates finished products from raw materials. It may sell to a reseller or directly to the customer. Think Apple, Coca-Cola, Christian Dior, Toyota, General Electric, Exxon, Huawei, etc.

Distributor

A distributor buys products in bulk from manufacturers or growers and resells them to retailers or the public. Think: auto dealerships, electronics stores, pharmaceutical distributors, food wholesalers, etc.

Aggregator

The aggregator business model is a recently updated model where the company leverages various service providers of a certain niche and sell their services under its brand. The company pays the service providers a fixed fee or a portion of the revenue. Think: Uber, Lyft, Instacart, Airbnb, Oyo, etc. yoli, a company I co-founded in 2015 with Luke Priddy is also a leading example of this model for online education in China

Direct to consumer model

In the manufacturer to consumer "direct model" reach buyers directly and compress the distribution channel resulting in the removal of intermediaries in a supply chain (e.g., distributor, wholesaler, broker, or agent) by "cutting out the middleman" in this model companies deal with every customer directly, for example via the Internet, retails stores or both. Think: Amazon.com, Alibaba, Dell Computer, Apple, etc.

Retailer (or e-commerce Retailer)

A retailer purchases products from a distributor or wholesaler and sells directly to the public. Think: WalMart, Tesco, etc. This can include e-commerce retailers like Amazon.com as well. From 2017, Amazon.com is beginning to open retail stores to display offline a portion of the wares it sells online. It is also experimenting with un-manned retail convenience stores as are Alibaba, JD.com and several sizeable Chinese internet retailers. This space is experiencing a lot of change and innovation now.

Clicks and Mortar

Is a company that has both an online and offline presence allowing its customers to shop online and then chooses to have the products delivered or pick up products from the physical stores. Think: WalMart, Sephora, Target, Bed Bath & Beyond, etc.

Affiliate

In contrast to the Clicks and Mortar site, which seeks to drive a high volume of traffic to one site (online or physical), the affiliate model, provides purchase opportunities wherever people may be. This is accomplished by offering financial incentives (in the form of a percentage of revenue) to affiliated partners. Think: Amazon marketplace, Rakuten, eBay, terraleads, Google, Facebook, etc.

Franchise

A franchise is a ready-made business that any qualified person can buy into. In return for the upfront payment and ongoing royalties or profit sharing, the franchisee is allowed to use a successful existing business model and brand. While the most famous franchises are all food-related retailers, the franchise business model is used in many industry segments. Think: McDonald's, KFC, Pizza Hut, GNC Fitness, etc.

Nickel-and-dime

In this model, the primary product is very cost-sensitive and is priced as low as possible. For all ancillary services that come with it, a separate amount is charged. Think: All low-cost air carriers, shared working spaces, etc.

Freemium

This is one of the most prevalent business models on the Internet. With the freemium business model companies offer basic online services, or a basic digital product, for free, while charging a premium for advanced or special features. Think: DropBox, LinkedIn, Spotify, most mobile App or game companies including Yodo1 which I co-founded with Henry Fong and is now the largest private publisher of mobile phone games in China.

Subscription

An extremely popular model these days for Internet-based services. A customer buys to initiate the service period, and the provider gets recurring revenues from them through fixed and repeat fees. The revenue stream remains intact until the customer formally "opts out." Think: Netflix, Netsuite, Adobe Creative Cloud, Apple Music, etc. An edutech company I co-founded in 2015 called yoli also employs this business model.

Pay what you can (PWYC)

A non-profit or for-profit business model which does not depend on set prices for what it sells, but instead asks customers to pay what they feel the product or service is worth to them. This model depends on community reciprocity and trust to succeed. Sometimes users pay with their time instead of money to make the product better for all. Think: freeware software (donationware), Metropolitan Museum of Art, bloggers, open source software such as Redhat, Apache, Hadoop, etc.

Pay what you want (PWYW)

Similar to PWYC is sometimes used synonymously, but "pay what you want" is more about paying what you think something is worth and also on your ability to pay. Think: RedCross, Kickstarter, Fundly, Kiva, etc.

Value-added reseller model

Value Added Reseller (VAR) is a business that makes something which is resold by other companies with customizations that add value to the original product or service. These modifications often industry-specific in nature and are essential for the distribution. Companies who want to leverage a VAR model have to develop a VAR network. The VAR model has been adopted by many Technology companies especially enterprise software that requires customization for the customer's specific needs. Think: IBM Global Services, Accenture, TATA, Unisys, etc.

High Touch

The High Touch model requires a skilled sales force to close the sale. Overall revenues of the company are highly dependent on the relationship between the salesperson and the customer. Companies with this business model operate on relationships, trust, and credibility. Think: IBM, EMC, VMWare, Salesforce.com, SAP, Oracle, etc.

Low Touch

Contrary to the High Touch model, the Low Touch model requires minimal human involvement in selling a product or service. The lack of a sales force results in low cost of sale but may require significant R&D investment to improve sales automation further while improving customer experience.

Think: Ikea, ZenDesk, MailChimp, SurveyMonkey, machine translation services, etc.

Brokerage

Market-makers who bring buyers and sellers together and facilitate transactions, Brokers take a percentage of the transaction or membership fees or both. Think E*Trade, Charles Schwab, Experian, Axiom, Fiverr, etc.

Advertising

The Internet advertising model is a logical extension of the traditional media broadcast model to online. Think Google, Facebook, WPP, Omnicom, digital marketing firms, etc.

Infomediary

Companies using this model collect and package data useful to consumers when considering a purchase. Some firms function as infomediaries (information intermediaries) assisting buyers or sellers understand a given market. Think Yelp.com, Zillow.com, Consumer Reports, Reputation.com, etc.

Wikipedia is a reasonably good source for basic information on business model types. However, since the Internet and mobile connectivity has spawned so many new business models, the information on them is becoming dated. That doesn't mean business models are outdated—no that would never happen—but it means that categorization is more important than definitions. Recently, the discussion has centered more around "Platform" type than "Business Model" type. However, each platform has an inherent business model tied to it. Following is a fairly recent overview of platform types on the Internet with specific company examples:

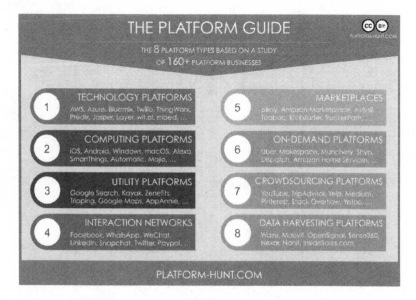

So, as said previously, in the early stages of a startup you should spend time on what I call the "inverted T." These are the core areas (value proposition, revenue, costs) you need to have mastered when recruiting co-founders, investors, etc. It is true that with a startup the "the plan will always be wrong and will evolve," doesn't mean you should spend no time working on it. This is a chance for the team to put their minds together and visualize all possible scenarios and discuss which ones are most probable. Most first-time entrepreneurs have huge blind spots. Do the "inverted T" and then do the rest of the Business Model Canvas early in the startup gestation and revisit it often. You need to understand and be able to articulate your startup's business model in your sleep. Define it, understand it, work it.

Now that you understand the Business Model Canvas let us focus on the real meat of this chapter and this book: the

Minimum Viable Product (MVP). Gone is the wild and crazy Internet Bubble of 1999 and the time when it wasn't deemed necessary to have a clear way to monetize your idea. Companies formed during that time that didn't figure out how to monetize all failed eventually. Even Google, Facebook and many other companies who went after a "acquire users first, figure out how to monetize" later strategy were only able to become valuable companies and go public through effective monetization of their ad traffic. Even YouTube, once the last bastion of "free" content, encourages you to pay to turn off ads so you can watch the videos you like. For every good idea that becomes a real company, there is always a good monetization strategy.

"Startup success can be engineered by following the process, which means it can be learned, which means it can be taught." - Eric Ries

---

When I first came across the term Minimum Viable Product (MVP) as documented in Eric Ries seminal book "The Lean Startup" the first time, I felt it was more of a product manager's wet dream rather than a full-blown process for creating a viable product from an idea and a team. After some thought, though, I came to see MVP as standing for the "Minimum Valuable Product" or the minimum product that people will consider valuable enough to buy. But regardless of how you care to define the acronym, the main point is that MVP is the first product you as a founding team will put out in the marketplace. Therefore you need to define it quickly, set a target date for shipping it and gear all your efforts around doing this one thing, right. Building the MVP is your first "crunch time" as a startup. You will be tempted to add features, avoid the hard technical issues, extend the deadline and all manner of things. As a team, you must not fall prey to these temptations. Become fanatical about your product and the launch date. If you find that as a team you can not meet the MVP goals you have set for your startup, the issues are more likely with your team and execution capability. If you miss your MVP date and targets, you need to seriously consider shelving the project, pivoting quickly or changing/augmenting the founding team. All of these will have implications affecting time-to-market, team confidence and your burn rate.

An MVP needs to be boiled down and refined until it meets the following four criteria:

After mentoring hundreds of entrepreneurs, I find the Minimum Viable Product (MVP) process first described by Eric Ries invaluable to ensuring that entrepreneurs get their priorities right from the beginning and avoid costly and time-wasting mistakes. A core concept of the MVP process is the build-measure-learn feedback loop. The MVP definition happens between the "Ideas" circle and the "Build" circle. So as you can see defining your MVP is the next thing you do after deciding to explore turning an idea into a startup.

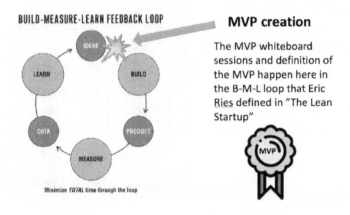

MVP creation

The MVP whiteboard sessions and definition of the MVP happen here in the B-M-L loop that Eric Ries defined in "The Lean Startup"

To build a great company you need to turn the idea into a product or a highly scalable service. That is what the founding team should all be signed up for. To do this effectively the team needs to be aligned with a singular vision, and each member needs to deliver on what he/she is responsible for delivering. Doing this is hard, but it is what makes the startup experience unique, unforgettable and, yes, fun! You will create something that has only existed previously as an idea and turn it into a product/service many (hopefully millions) of people will pay for. In the early days of your product, the founders will inevitably be spending most of their time on building and refining the product. That is why having a clear, mutually agreed upon MVP that is written down is absolutely crucial to avoid wasting valuable time, money and effort.

As a startup founder, your mission is to build something (product, service or some combination thereof) that a small number of users love. It should solve a real problem for them and make them so happy that they want to tell others about it. If your startup makes something only a few people like, or find novel, you will fail. At the same time, you need to build a product quickly and put it in front of those users who will love it. This means the product will have enough features to make them love it but most certainly won't have all of them. This is the essence of the MVP. Building just enough of the product to get early, passionate users to pay while giving you feedback on how and what you need to do to make the product better and more able to address a broader, much larger audience.

I also firmly believe that the ability to create (first on a whiteboard, then on documented on "paper," and finally a real product) an MVP offering that people will spend money to buy is the critical first execution hurdle of a startup's founding team. With my startups and in my mentoring practice I will often guide a startup team through the phases of building an MVP (from whiteboard to paper) and then if during the process it becomes clear that the idea has issues we will either decide whether or not to shelve the project. It is much better to spend two days to a week in intense MVP sessions and decide not to move forward than to skip the MVP mapping process and waste potentially years of your life on something that was flawed, to begin with.

So how minimal should the MVP be? According to Eric Ries "Probably much more minimum than you think." I agree fully with this statement. The minimal product, experience or service that can be built to get a fanatical user to pay something for it should be your MVP. Following is the template I use in my MVP workshops to help entrepreneurs prepare for their "MVP whiteboard weekends."

Work in workshop #2

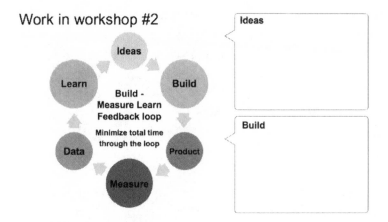

Ideas

Build

Reid Hoffman, prolific Silicon Valley early stage investor and founder of LinkedIn, often says, "If your product isn't embarrassing when you launch it, you've launched it too late." Don't be a perfectionist. Put your product out there. Tell people about it. Encourage them to give you feedback. That way they can help you make it better. Very rarely is the market exactly as you perceive it to be. Relentlessly pursue feedback and challenge your assumptions. Making the necessary changes to your product when it is an MVP will save you lots of valuable time and energy. Lose your ego regarding your product. It won't help you. You may ask: But what if the customer hates my product? What about customer retention? These things will get better over time, and you can iterate through them. Your main goal at this point has to be on getting those customers. Although it may be counter-intuitive, like Airbnb, Google, and Facebook before you spend the minimum amount of time and money in product development and the maximum in channeling customers to the product. That is the only way to get the valuable market feedback you need to improve the product (or build the right product). You need to know that your product is viable (and valuable) first--once you have determined that beyond a doubt, you can shift to a focus on quality and customer retention. I am not suggesting you build an awful product, but as Reid Hoffman says you should be somewhat embarrassed about it. Embarrassed that the UI kind of sucks or some of the functionality is lacking, etc. The fact is your early adopters won't care. If you are truly solving a pain point for them or making them happy, they will forgive the blemishes and the defects inherent in an early version. This is counter-intuitive, I know. Most people take a craftsman mentality for granted and insist you "should be proud of what you do, and therefore you should do it as well as you can." Long term I agree. However, the tailor, hat maker or jewelry designer did not always make products this good. They iterated to a level of craftsmanship. They put the time in to perfect their craft. You are validating a market. You are innovating. You should not aim for a perfect product in the first rev. It is not only unrealistic; it is counterproductive to do so. Focus on solving the customer problem and be proud of your product and business in the long term.

Only 2 Reasons Customers Buy From You

1. **Increase pleasure** (e.g. glowing health, freedom, comfort, popularity, better earning ability, good looks, quench hunger/thirst)
2. **Solving a problem** or pain point so they can be happy again (e.g. stress, financial problems, poor health, upward mobility, communication, etc.)

That is it. Only two reasons! Easy enough, right. Not Exactly...

What is your VALUE PROPOSITION? Validate it rigorously on the criteria above. Then visualize it as a flow (and a product or service)

Actually getting product/market fit right takes lots of trial and error, willful stubbornness and perseverance.

Also, an MVP is not always a fully functional product. In many cases, it can be an effective preview of what is to come. For example, the following are a combination of my own efforts and some of the more classic industry examples:

A Video on a Crowdsourcing Site

Hundreds of thousands of other entrepreneurs and I have had success selling products and services before they are even built by leveraging platforms like Kickstarter, IndieGoGo and RocketHub. I have raised 10's of thousands of dollars selling products and services myself and my co-founders were planning to build by creating a compelling video and placing it on Kickstarter. The time it took me to write this book you are reading now was entirely funded on Kickstarter as part of a campaign for one of my startups. The same result can be achieved with a video on YouTube or other video sharing site that contains a link to a page where you can transact and sell the product or service to be delivered at a date in the future.

KICKSTARTER

yoli: fund your dream lifestyle

yoli - make money anytime anywhere by tutoring others on your smartphone

Created by
James LaLonde

76 backers pledged ¥1,037,809 to help bring this project to life.

A Landing Page

For a brand new product or service businesses especially, a website landing page is enough to begin attracting paid customers. This is another technique I have used many times in the past. A "landing page" is a website where potential customers "land" after clicking a link from a video, an online ad (e.g., Facebook or Google) and email, banner, scanning a QR code or other type of campaign. Invest in a landing page and some Search Engine Optimization (SEO), so you can test what potential customers will respond to. The testing you do (see "A/B testing" described later in this chapter) will give you three critical pieces of information: What attracts your customers? How much does it cost (in advertising spend) to get them to click on something? Also, how much they are willing to pay? In this way, you can estimate the viability of your business.

This is how Google started out. Their MVP was the beta version of their Stanford University search engine project, and an email subscribe function.

A Combined Landing Page and Compelling Video

Perhaps the most famous (and most effective) example of selling the concept of an MVP before completely building the fully featured final product was the Dropbox example. Because the market was unknown, and the technical challenge of building out a fully functional platform for cloud-based seamless file backup and synchronization across Windows, Mac, and Linux was huge, Drew Houston the CEO and founder of Dropbox decided to first create a simple service and a simple 3 minute video to show how it would work. The video made something hard and inherently technically advanced look effortless. Within 24 hours they had 75,000 people on their beta waiting list.

Store, Sync and Share your files online.

Download Dropbox   Watch the Video

Want to find out more? Take a quick tour!

Available for Windows, Mac and Linux

Contact Us · Feedback · Press · Partnerships

Flintstoning

Named after the cartoon series where the family "drives around" in what looks to be an automobile but is a wood and stone constructed facsimile that Fred Flintstone powers with his feet. In the startup world "flintstoning" is when your product or service lacks a function but you can make up for it by doing it manually.

Image copyright: Hanna-Barbera Products, Inc.

In practice, "Flintstoning" could mean that you do certain things that all users expect manually until you have the time and budget to code them. For example, password reset, unsubscribe, or other processes that you can do manually until you set up an automated system that handles these requests. In the early days when the number of users is small, you can usually get away with these things to make your ship dates. At yoli, while we planned to have 300+ lessons, we didn't want to commit to writing all of them until we had feedback from students and the process was field tested. So in the first few months, we got by on 100 or so lessons and make it a requirement for students to take them in order. That decision bought us three months to write the rest of the curriculum and field test and refine the first hundred lessons. This was not an issue for our students, and it allowed us to make our ship date.

Flintstoning can also mean manually executing a process that can be automated later if the product or service takes off. A famous example of this is Zappos the successful online shoe seller that was snapped up eventually by Amazon for 1.2 billion. In the beginning, Zappos wasn't sure who would be buying how much of what so there was no sense in filling up a warehouse full of shoes and building a state-of-the-art e-commerce backend. Instead, the founder went to local shoe shops and asked the owner's permission to take photos of shoes and put them online. Once the orders started coming in, he went to the shop, bought the pair that was ordered, shipped it, handled payments, returns, etc., all of it himself, and by hand. Not very scalable but it helped Zappos validate the market before too much was invested up front in stock and warehouses.

A Sign-Up Form

A sign-up form is a way to judge if a particular product or feature can create enough interest before you build it. Both LinkedIn and GoogleMail used this technique to create an early set of users prior to the product being anywhere near completed or spec'd out. In the case of LinkedIn, it was especially effective as you couldn't be invited to use it (in the future) unless one of your friends forwarded the link to you. Given the platform itself was predicated on a network effect being in place, it was nothing short of ingenious.

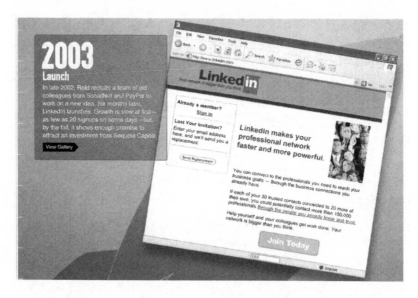

A/B Testing On Facebook or other Social Media sites

Apparently, Tim Ferriss wanted to title his first book "Broadband and White Sand." He ended up calling it "The 4-Hour Work Week: Escape 9-5, Live Anywhere, and Join the New Rich". The result is it sold millions of copies. I bought that book the month it came out. Had it been named "Broadband and White Sand" perhaps none of us would even know who Tim Ferris is today.

According to the story I heard, to settle the debate between his publisher and himself on what to call the book, they decided to do a few Internet ads to test title names. I think you know what they found out. A few hundred dollars spent on testing a few different names on the Internet and monitoring the clickthru performance launched Tim's career. This "A/B Testing" is pretty easy to do, and there are plenty of websites that can take you through the process. I use this method a lot personally and highly recommend it.

Podcast As A Market Primer

While it is probably not the first thing you would think of, a podcast can be an excellent way to launch a product or service. If you want to create a following and establish credibility in a field a podcast is an extremely inexpensive way to potentially reach a core audience, and if combined with a subscriber mailing list you can test topics, concepts and ideas and by monitoring the stats can see what interests your audience. Many authors use podcasts for building their brands and for service offerings a podcast can be an extremely effective way of keeping your audience abreast of the market and startup's new and upcoming offerings. I recently co-founded a consulting startup that leveraged a bilingual podcast to develop a business helping Chinese companies partner with foreign companies and Foreign companies partner with Chinese companies as China expands its trade and digital infrastructure worldwide via the Belt and Road Initiative

The podcast was vital to establishing the company's credibility by having famous and interesting guests come on and give their insights. Unlike most other podcasts we focused on being bilingual (offering each podcast in English and Chinese) and built a strong following in both China and all over the world. Furthermore, because the podcast format requires that you meet or at least record an actual interview, we were able to get to know the key players in the industry faster and better than we would have if we had waited for them to discover our website.

VOICES OF THE
BELT & ROAD
一 带 一 路 之 声

Teaser Mini App or Game

While there are examples all over the world, one particular country where the concept of using a Mini App or a Mini Game to promote a full-fledged App or Game in China. In July of 2018, Google made quite a splash by releasing it's "Guess My Sketch" WeChat Mini Game on WeChat in China. Prior to this Google had 50 million hand-drawn sketches in its AI database for picture recognition research. By releasing this App on WeChat, Google will very quickly grow that number by an order of magnitude given WeChat's huge and active user base of 1 billion people. Google which had been officially "out" of the China market made it clear with this Mini-Game App that they were coming back to China in a small, yet big way.

While some of these techniques may seem unnecessary or even gimmicky, they are invaluable for helping entrepreneurs avoid wasted time, effort and money building the wrong product. In 2010, Drew Houston of Dropbox summed it up nicely in one slide:

What we learned

- Biggest risk: making something no one wants
- Not launching → painful, but not learning → fatal
- Put something in users hands (doesn't have to be code) and get real feedback ASAP
- Know where your target audience hangs out & speak to them in an authentic way

The MVP process that I use (see below) is extremely powerful as it allows you to test the idea and the execution ability of the founding team before a single line of code is written. Make a good MVP, that customers will love and talk about. Startup success is not a money raising contest. Very few startups die from competition or because some other company raised more money. Startups fail because they don't end up building products that customers absolutely love. Think about the first version of Google search. They spent zero time on the interface; they just focused on bringing the best Internet search results to the user in the shortest amount of time. The rest of what they do came later after they had all those users who loved and trusted them. The MVP process is first and foremost the forum for a startup team to define what matters most and what is the minimum functionality required to make a few people love the product enough to pay money and tell friends about it.

My "Whiteboard Weekend" MVP Creation Process

I highly suggest locking yourself and your co-founders in a room with a whiteboard for a weekend to flesh out your MVP. Even if the founders live in different countries, cities it is essential you come together face-to-face at least once before doing the startup. There are things about meeting physically that you can learn about a person that you simply can't base solely on a phone call or talking head on a video call. I have started companies with people I didn't know well and had never met. However, I have always kicked off the MVP process with a face-to-face meeting. If you come out of the room feeling more excited about the idea, then you did going in, that is a good sign you have a viable startup on your hands.

Once you have decided it makes sense to seriously consider doing a startup you need to focus on defining your MVP. I would never do a startup without an MVP. Here's why, and what a solid MVP allows you to do:

- It will enable you to test a core set of functionalities before you commit to the expense and effort of building the full product. By offering an initial set of core features rather than a feature-complete product, you can collect user information, get your product to market quickly and keep costs down.

- It allows you to improve our product-to-market fit in real time. Because you have real, paying customers the feedback you get from them on what features they use most and least, how much time they spend using the product is invaluable. This feedback allows your team to prioritize functionality for future iterations of the product properly.

- It's a cost-efficient, pay as you go approach. Because MVPs are created iteratively over a period of time, the cost is spread out, and the size of the revenue generated increases with each new customer and functionality upgrade.

Pre MVP Whiteboard Weekend Prep

Together

- Write down your value proposition (see above for definition)

- Write down your target market

- Discuss the user flow and the touchpoints in the solution

- Discuss pricing and cost in a general sense

Individually

- Validate Customer Segments (each person pitch the idea to at least ten people who could be potential customers or who have experience in the market space you plan to target)

- Validate Technical Viability (What technology platforms do you think fit best? Has something similar been done before or are you in the uncharted technical territory? Does the technical talent to pull it off reside in the founding team or not?)

- Do SWOTs on competitors or comparables. Each person should do a few.

- Create a business model canvas for the company

The MVP Whiteboard Weekend

- Discuss the business model. Compare the business model canvasses that each founder did as part of his/her homework. Review and discuss the value proposition. Each founder should take a shot at articulating it verbally in the room until it feels right.

- Whiteboard the product technical design and UI.

- Set goals for the MVP and for what you can accomplish in 4-6 weeks that would prove or disprove your business model (user growth, revenue, funding). What is the scope of the MVP's functionality? How much will you charge and how will you actively collect feedback from the early users? What is your sales goal for the MVP level product?

- Similarly, establish the goals and assumptions for the startup. I like to collectively come up with 5-7 "mantras" that define what kind of company we are, what we stand for. These form the foundation of company culture, and by referring to them when disputes arise, they help avoid unnecessary conflicts and dissension.

- Discuss the feature set for the MVP. Discuss the list of possible features that should be included in the MVP. Later you can prioritize and lock down the final prioritized feature set. For each unique feature, discuss the following:

o   How "sticky" is this feature? Does it make users want to come back?

o   How often will the feature be used?

o   How much revenue or customer satisfaction value does the feature bring?

o   How risky (technically or profit margin-wise) is the feature?

Lock down the GUI look and feel and the product "flow."

- Discuss, define and document the main user flow in the product looks like and how most customers will use the software application. What problem are you solving and how (and in how many steps)?

- The "flow" is the path the user takes as he/she navigates through the product. This should also be discussed, mapped out, drawn on the whiteboard and later explicitly documented.

Do a "Pre Mortem"

o   Discuss how you would roll out the product or service offering and what things, events, situations could cause the product to fail (refer to the premortem section later in this chapter).

o   Focus on show-stoppers. Only focus on solving problems absolutely critical to your project. In other words, if the problem occurs, will it dramatically impact the project? If the answer is no, cross it out; it doesn't belong on your pre-mortem list. Adhering to this rule of thumb will eliminate many of the non-mission critical issues.

- o Pick problems that are likely to occur. Only spend time on the real hard problems, the ones everyone was secretly worried about but never brought up until now.

- o Discard problems you have no control over. Every project will face some external risks that you can't control. Forget those for now because there's nothing you can do about them. From here on out, you're focusing on problems you can actually fix prior to launching the MVP.

Decide on your values, define your culture, write your "Mantras"

- I always make it a practice to define "what we stand for" when I start a company. I always suggest this to the people I mentor and those who attend my MVP workshops. The reason I do this is because building the MVP is the first real project the founding team will complete together. This first effort will test the team's individual capabilities as well as their ability to work as a team. It will most probably be the hardest task in the early life of the startup.

- The mantras are the startup's core values. When faced with indecision on which path to take in the future, you will find yourself coming back to and reviewing these. These mantras, if each founder takes them to heart, become the cultural foundation of the startups. Below is an example of the mantras of one of my startups: yoli

 The 7 yoli Company Mantras

1. **Assume people are reliable**. This means that the company can rely on people (teachers and students) to perform the tasks they are given. If they can't perform a task, the company will examine what circumstances impede them and what it can do to overcome those obstacles.
2. **Offer fewer,more relevant options**. We are fanatical about knowing our students and what is good for them. Any service that does not provide value to students is not done. We have a responsibility to ensure the best service offerings are offered to our students in a timely fashion.
3. **We constantly look for opportunities to reduce waste** in services and processes.
4. **Do it right the first time**—we strive for zero unsatisfied students
5. **Everything can be improved.** Each service offering and process will be continuously reviewed and improved using scientific methods and thinking. (e.g. process improvement and product improvement involve generating hypotheses, conducting experiments, collecting data, reviewing the results, and then implementing change.
6. **Be a responsible company** to our students, teachers and the community. We obey the law.
7. **Convince, don't defeat.** We must explain the reasoning behind our policies, convincing one's colleagues rather than defeating them. Gaining consensus is preferable to winning the argument.

Other things you need to do during or right after your MVP weekend

- Based on the whiteboard drawings one of the founding team members should mock up the basic GUI and layout for the product and come to an agreement. The mockup should be done so that it is at a level that can be presented to an investor using Adobe XD, Photoshop or PowerPoint

- Brainstorm regarding the best channels to test your value proposition.

- Decide to create a basic landing page for a campaign test. Discuss a campaign to drive traffic to the landing page

- Decide which parts of the product/service to build out in the MVP phase and which parts to "Flintstone," e.g., develop a plan to deliver some of the services without software. What resources would you need? How far can it scale without automation?

- Review the fulfillment model and the user flow for the product/service. Identify potential pain points and ways to resolve.

- Discuss how you get paid and the process to support it.

- Discuss how you will make the product "sticky" and how you will retain customers. Do you have a well-defined upgrade path for power users?

- Social Media. How do you plan to market and how will you encourage your customers to share their positive experiences. Should you create case studies based on early users?

- What will the expected Lifetime Value (LTV) of your average customer? What are the assumptions behind that number? How can you increase it with more functionality or a smoother user experience over time?

- Review assumptions in the financial model especially costs and revenues. Someone on the team needs to be responsible for doing an update model post MVP weekend for the founding team to review

- Discuss the long-term vision for the startup. What does the world look like five years, two years, one year, and six months from now? Write it down

Don't be afraid to be ambitious with the MVP but do be realistic. If the MVP is too simple or easy to build, you risk not thoroughly testing your market hypothesis and getting false hope early. The MVP should challenge the team's capabilities but should also be realistically doable in the time frame set. It is a known fact that setting and achieving ambitious goals is intrinsically more satisfying.

EDWIN LOCKE, THE PATRIARCH OF STRUCTURED GOAL SETTING, MINED A DOZEN STUDIES FOR A QUANTITATIVE CORRELATION BETWEEN GOAL DIFFICULTY AND ACHIEVEMENT. THE ARENAS RANGED WIDELY, BUT THE RESULTS WERE "UNEQUIVOCAL," LOCKE WROTE. "THE HARDER THE GOAL, THE HIGHER THE LEVEL OF PERFORMANCE. . . . ALTHOUGH SUBJECTS WITH VERY HARD GOALS REACHED THEIR GOALS FAR LESS OFTEN THAN SUBJECTS WITH VERY EASY GOALS, THE FORMER CONSISTENTLY PERFORMED AT A HIGHER LEVEL THAN THE LATTER." THE STUDIES FOUND THAT "STRETCHED" WORKERS WERE NOT ONLY MORE PRODUCTIVE BUT MORE MOTIVATED AND ENGAGED: "SETTING SPECIFIC CHALLENGING GOALS IS ALSO A MEANS OF ENHANCING TASK INTEREST AND OF HELPING PEOPLE TO DISCOVER THE PLEASURABLE ASPECTS OF AN ACTIVITY." DOERR, JOHN. MEASURE WHAT MATTERS: HOW GOOGLE, BONO, AND THE GATES FOUNDATION ROCK THE WORLD WITH OKRS (P. 187). PENGUIN PUBLISHING GROUP.

MINIMUM VIABLE PRODUCT

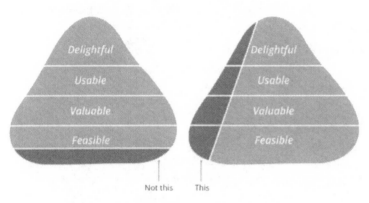

Graphic by Deloitte University Press

Your early users will be your fanatics, your testers, your window to the larger world. So you need to be completely hands-on with them. Get to know them, meet them, ask them for help and referrals, ask their opinions on features, functionality, UI, and flow. If they have questions or problems, great founders are always first to respond. At the beginning of a startup, you need to do things that are hands-on and don't scale. Reid Hoffman's podcast "Masters of Scale" is one I love, and he launched the podcast by talking about how in the early days you need to do things that don't scale. He spoke with founders of Airbnb about how they went about taking care of their first hosts and users.

"It's really hard to get even ten people to love anything, but it's not hard if you spend a ton of time with them." Airbnb co-founder Brian Chesky

With yoli, the on-demand language learning platform I co-founded we treated our first ten then 100 users even better than we treated ourselves. We met with them in person, talked to them daily, ate dinner with them, sang Karaoke with them and generally made them friends for life. And it was those people and their love for us and the platform that got us to the first 1,000 students and then 10,000 and so on. They told us what we needed to do to make the platform better and all the while telling everyone they knew how great we were. Moreover, because we listened to them, they cheered us through each incremental product improvement.

Making this product feedback look tight and responding quickly breeds passion amongst your user base and also makes your product better much faster. Do everything you can to ensure there are no layers between you and the core customer base that will give you the feedback you need. Make it easy for your users to help you make the product better.

In this "matrix of knowledge," the four quadrants represent the following:

A. What you know that you know,

B. What you don't know that you know,

C. What you know that you don't know

D. What you don't know that you don't know.

MATRIX OF KNOWLEDGE

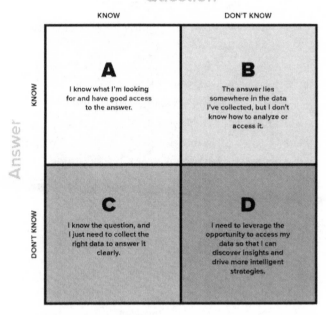

Graphic courtesy of Umbel

When you start to evaluate an idea and think about forming it into an MVP, you will definitely be operating in quadrant A, leveraging the things you already know. Also, being the smart person you are you will proactively working quadrant C by talking to people and asking questions you don't yet know the answer for. If you do the premortem I suggested above then you will begin to enter the realm of quadrant B and come up with some questions you don't know the answer to and start working on those. However, if you create your MVP right, it will take you into the land of quadrant D by turning up things (questions, answers, situations) you never expected at all. How you react to these quadrant D issues is going to have a huge effect on the success of your startup.

"BLACK SWAN LOGIC MAKES WHAT YOU DON'T KNOW FAR MORE RELEVANT THAN WHAT YOU DO KNOW. CONSIDER THAT MANY BLACK SWANS CAN BE CAUSED AND EXACERBATED BY THEIR BEING UNEXPECTED. THINK OF THE TERRORIST ATTACK OF SEPTEMBER 11, 2001: HAD THE RISK BEEN REASONABLY CONCEIVABLE ON SEPTEMBER 10, IT WOULD NOT HAVE HAPPENED. IF SUCH A POSSIBILITY WERE DEEMED WORTHY OF ATTENTION, FIGHTER PLANES WOULD HAVE CIRCLED THE SKY ABOVE THE TWIN TOWERS, AIRPLANES WOULD HAVE HAD LOCKED BULLETPROOF DOORS, AND THE ATTACK WOULD NOT HAVE TAKEN PLACE, PERIOD. SOMETHING ELSE MIGHT HAVE TAKEN PLACE. WHAT? I DON'T KNOW." TALEB, NASSIM NICHOLAS. THE BLACK SWAN: SECOND EDITION: THE IMPACT OF THE HIGHLY IMPROBABLE. RANDOM HOUSE PUBLISHING GROUP.

I want to take you through a scenario I experienced and how it pays to think about the things you definitely don't know the answer for, and you likely don't even know to be asking a question about. That quadrant D stuff that bestselling author Nassib Nicholas Taleb calls "anti-knowledge."

Image courtesy of Whitehotpix via Zuma Press

One of the things I like most about Beijing is that it's flat, and if you have a bicycle, you can almost get anywhere faster than you can in a car given the traffic. Although I had been traveling to the city nearly monthly for business for many years, when I finally moved there in 2013 I started looking for the perfect bicycle. Being American, I first bought a car but soon found out I couldn't bear the traffic that meant I spent the better part of every day inside my car instead of in the meetings the traffic inevitably made me late for.

For those of you who are unfamiliar with the city, the traffic in Beijing is so bad that it made the history books in 2015 (see photo above) and in 2010 for an October holiday backup that was 62 miles in length at its worst point and lasted some 12 days. So in 2015 when I started mentoring an exciting company called Tsinova that had a young CEO and a great founding team all from top-tier Tsinghua University. Tsinova's mission was to build the ultimate battery assisted commuting bicycle for Chinese cities. The CEO had gone to work for Audi right out of university and had an impeccable design pedigree. He also had the focus and passion I like to see in a young CEO. They made a stylish, yet affordable and extremely practical bicycle and had really mastered the supply chain out of Shenzhen, so they were testing and prototyping at an amazing pace.

What's more, they had partnered with upscale retail locations, eateries and done lots of events to garner fans. Pre-launch they had nearly 10,000 pre-orders for the bicycle. They were doing everything right and with the government regulations to ban gas powered and eventually larger electrical scooters coming within months they were the only company on the market with a stylish, pedal plus electric (battery-assisted) bicycle on the market. With my help, they had also set up distributors in Japan and California. This company was going places—or so it seemed. Having lived myself for many years in Tokyo where the vast majority of bicycles were and are already battery assisted, I saw this company as the perfect vehicle to bring that successful model to China. I was so convinced of the concept and so personally involved and excited about the company myself; I had already planned to invest in their Series B round.

Then the Black Swan event happened. And boy did things change quickly.

The sudden rise of WeChat as a payment platform made it possible for a company called Mobike with the same sense of design and sustainability to enter the market with a superbly-designed commuter bike that you didn't have to buy, you just rented by the mile. And the price was oh so cheap. You could use the Mobike every day for a few years to commute and not even come close to what you would spend on the 2,000 RMB plus Tsinova bicycle. And not only did you not have to buy the Mobike but when you were finished riding you could just leave it where you got off and forget about it. Overnight it seemed the bikes were available on any street corner and as long as you had a smartphone, WeChat and 1 RMB (which all 1.4 billion people in China do) then the bike was yours for your commute.

What is a BLACK SWAN?

A BLACK SWAN is a highly improbable event with three principal characteristics: It is unpredictable; it carries a massive impact; and, after the fact, we concoct an explanation that makes it appear less random, and more predictable, than it was.

The sudden death of the just-launched Tsinova bicycle was swift and merciless. Literally overnight everyone in Beijing and most large Chinese cities stopped buying bicycles for commuting. Within a year the newly minted Unicorn startups like Mobike, Ofo and 30 other less well funded local competitors were so dominant that new bicycle sales at retail stores literally ceased. People started seeing the bicycle as something like air, water, and electricity. Today if you search for Tsinova on the Internet you can find the last, best version of their website which has not been taken down but you can't find them for sale. What you can find is people who did buy them complaining on some public forums that the company abandoned them and they have no way to get their bicycles serviced or parts replaced.

For me this story is personal and represented a turning point in the way I think about startups. There were three main takeaways for me that I hope you will take to heart:

1) The pace of innovation and execution has increased well beyond anything humans have experienced before. China sets the pace of innovation worldwide now. The speed of innovation and the platforms available (Internet, Mobile, WeChat, AI, etc.) are such that a company with the right product at the right time with the right funding and business model can dominate extremely quickly. From a matter of decades when I was at Microsoft to a matter of half-decades with the advent Google and Facebook, to a matter of months which is what we see now with China's pace of innovation. According to the visionary Ray Kurzweil, civilizations advance by "repurposing" the ideas and breakthroughs of their predecessors. Similarly, each generation of technology builds on the advances of previous generations, and this creates a positive feedback loop of improvements. Kurzweil's big idea is that each new generation of technology stands on the shoulders of its predecessors—in this way, advances in technology enable the next generation of even better technology. What I have learned is that China is now standing on the shoulder of Silicon Valley and is leveraging past gains there to drive exponentially faster innovation in China. In the tech space, it is not just Silicon Valley that is driving innovation anymore. The whole world needs to start looking at China and what is happening here or risk being blindsided. Japan and Europe tend to follow US trends, but China is setting its own course and speed.

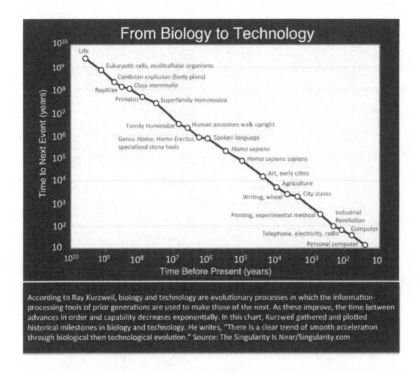

From Biology to Technology

According to Ray Kurzweil, biology and technology are evolutionary processes in which the information-processing tools of prior generations are used to make those of the next. As these improve, the time between advances in order and capability decreases exponentially. In this chart, Kurzweil gathered and plotted historical milestones in biology and technology. He writes, "There is a clear trend of smooth acceleration through biological then technological evolution." Source: The Singularity Is Near/Singularity.com

2) A platform adoption shift can wipe out everything that came before it. Tencent leveraged its success with the QQ instant messaging platform to build WeChat from scratch. WeChat quickly became a super app well beyond anything we have seen on the planet before with a billion people using it every day for all their communications, payments and work productivity needs. While mainly a China phenomenon and not well known in the West, basically you can look at all consumer and most B2B solutions in the lens of those that existed pre-WeChat and post-WeChat. While my first startup in China was in the mobile gaming space (iOS and Android), I quickly realized that WeChat was a game changer and all my subsequent startups have been built on top of WeChat. Even the game company I originally co-founded Yodo1 (now produces native games for the WeChat Mini Program platform). When you are founding a startup, you need to be extremely careful about what platform you choose to build your product/service on. In my career, I have successfully surfed the transitions from personal computing, local area networks, the Internet, cloud computing, mobile, mobile phone games and apps to WeChat apps and games.

As a good rule of thumb, proprietary technology must be at least ten times better than its closest substitute in some important dimension to lead to a real monopolistic advantage. Anything less than an order of magnitude better will probably be perceived as a marginal improvement and will be hard to sell, especially in an already crowded market." Thiel, Peter; Masters, Blake, Zero To One: Notes on Startups, or How to Build the Future (p. 48). The Crown Publishing Group

3) My rule of thumb is that **if the product does not represent 10x innovation, your customers will not change their old habits quickly, if ever.** Therefore even if you build a great product, you are always going to be exposed to Black Swan risk. If you are not doing something new and unique with regards to what is already out there, it is much better to spend your time finding a better startup idea than executing perfectly on one that is merely good. In my personal example above, Tsinova did everything right and executed flawlessly. However, that didn't prevent the company's product from being stillborn because as good as the execution was it was not a 10x innovation. They added a lightweight battery assist to a well-designed product and got it to market quickly, but it was still an incremental change. Ironically Peter Thiel's book had just come out in Chinese when I first met the CEO, and I gave him a copy as a present. I mentioned this "10x innovation" point to him and asked him to read the book, and we agreed we would find a time to

discuss it before I finalized my decision to invest or not. We never ended up discussing it. And I didn't invest in the company.

Success Through Understanding What Could Cause Failure

Shortly after the black swan bicycle episode, I related above I read Charlie Munger's Poor Charlie's Almanack. Before reading this book, I thought the entrepreneur's key to success was creating a vision, setting goals, and working hard toward them every day. If an entrepreneur failed, I thought it was because they did one of these steps wrong. The Tsinova and Mobike experience made me begin to doubt that hypothesis and everything I had believed regarding business up to now.

In the book Charlie Munger, Berkshire Hathaway vice chairman, and long-time Warren Buffett business partner shows another equally important path to success; proactively thinking through what can go wrong. That really jibed with the reality that I was finding in my daily existence in China was that things constantly go wrong no matter how smart and hardworking the people involved are.

In the book, Munger lays out how he continuously and methodically considers every way a plan could go wrong and plots out how to avoid each obstacle. He says: "Invert, always invert: Turn a situation or problem upside down. Look at it backward. What happens if all our plans go wrong? Where don't we want to go, and how do you get there? Instead of looking for success, make a list of how to fail instead—through sloth, envy, resentment, self-pity, entitlement, all the mental habits of self-defeat. Avoid these qualities, and you will succeed. Tell me where I'm going to die, so I don't go there."

Recently I have found that this approach helps entrepreneurs avoid roadblocks and be more prepared when you inevitably run into one. Furthermore, the concept of combining goal setting and obstacle avoidance is supported by over 100+ academic studies. The truth is if entrepreneurs only 'fantasize' about the future, they end up taking less preventative action than they would if they also spent the necessary time thinking what could go wrong and made plans to avoid it. So being a combination of both pessimistic and optimistic is better than just being optimistic. One of the best ways to win is not to lose.

To apply this to your startup follow these three steps with your co-founder(s):

1. List all possible situations in which the startup could possibly fail

2. Assign a numerical probability to each possibility and rank them from most to least likely

3. Brainstorm on preventative actions to avert the top 10 ways the startup could fail

4. Prioritize the actions that can be taken to avoid failure

If you have read (I not, I highly recommended that you do by the way) Daniel Kahneman's "Thinking Fast and Slow" you will learn that human beings are subject to numerous cognitive biases. Munger has been a student of these biases since before even Daniel Kahneman was born. One thing Munger proactively avoids in his decision-making are these biases—that more often than not can cause humans to make bad decisions. If you search Google or YouTube on either Charlie Munger or Daniel Kahneman, you will find a treasure trove of information to bring you up to speed on these biases, so I will leave you to it.

Today we are at once drowning in data and also learning how to leverage it to increase sales and usefulness to customers. Alibaba, Amazon, Tencent, Google, Facebook, they all do it. More and more these tools are becoming available to people with startup budgets. Seek them out and leverage them. Today companies who are strong at innovation are more than likely heavily relying on big data analytics and data mining than their counterparts who are less adept at innovating. Thinking about leveraging your startup's "big data" should happen from the beginning and way before your data is actually "big." The first step is visualizing exactly what type of data exist "out there."

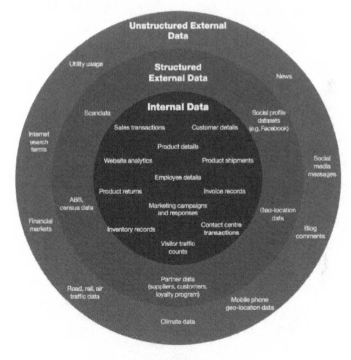

Source: PWC

From your first MVP Whiteboard Weekend until well beyond your first billion in sales you and the founding team need to continually ask yourselves what can you do to leverage consumer data in order to stumble upon the pivotal questions that you don't know yet to ask. Per Confucius, "True wisdom is knowing what you don't know."

How You and Your Co-Founding Team Can Find Out What You Don't Know

Most people are generally wired to think they pretty much know everything and what they don't know won't hurt them. That doesn't fly when you are doing a startup. It is actually most important to know what you don't know. While it is not possible to know everything, it is actually a very valuable exercise to try to catalog all the things you don't know and the areas where your knowledge is lacking. Since in a startup you are solving problems that have not existed previously, this kind of thinking will not only help your startup survive and thrive, but it will also give you the proper perspective to tackle unique problems you may not know you will be facing.

In my MVP workshops and mentoring sessions I often leverage a technique I learned from Skip Walter called the "Four Boxes of Knowing." I am almost hesitant to include it in this book because this exercise is so powerful when done live and I know that from here on out many people who attend my workshops will have already read this book.

In Skip's exercise, the facilitator starts out by describing "The Three Boxes of Knowing."

1.　　What you know

2.　　What do you know you don't know

3. What you don't know you don't know

On the whiteboard you draw something that looks like this:

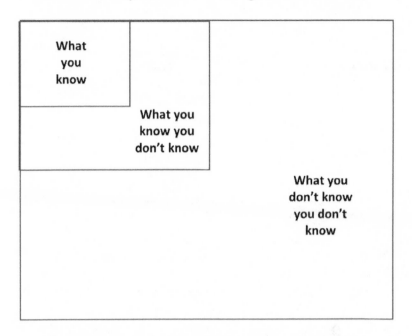

Then the facilitator asks "in this context, what is the fourth box of knowing?"

Of course, everyone immediately begins to add a larger fourth box to surround the other three and do the continued extension ad nauseum of "what you don't know that you don't know that you don't know …"

After a few questions to see if anyone has any other ideas, the facilitator draws in the smaller fourth box – what you think you know that is wrong.

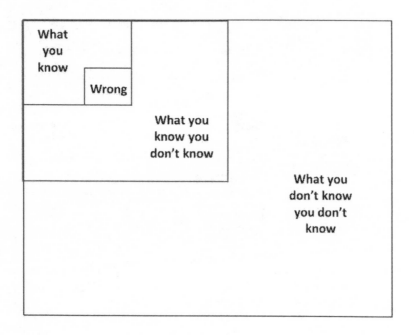

After a minute of laughing, the facilitator asks the group how they might go about learning something new. Exploring questions and thing that they don't know they don't know. Each participant is then asked to write some techniques or some examples of things they don't know they don't know. If properly facilitated this discussion becomes very lively, leveraging the group dynamics and the "wisdom of the crowd." And sometimes if the group has the right mix of people, some profound blind spots and unique speculations can come out of the largest box. It is this thinking that founders of startups need to proactively engage in to ensure they have the best chance to create a startup that will not only survive but thrive and grow spectacularly.

Pricing for your MVP

Pricing is a deep subject and would justify an entire book to discuss properly. What you charge and how you charge is closely tied to your business model (discussed earlier in this chapter) and your goals for the business (e.g., maximize profitability or maximize market coverage). I have had startups where we set the price once and leave it unchanged for years. I have also done startups where pricing was so sensitive in the marketplace that we felt the need to change them monthly, sometimes weekly. What pricing model you uses is highly relevant to the type of product/services your startup sells, the nature of the competitive and overall market situation. There is no one size fits all type advice regarding price.

When determining how to best price your products and services, consider:

Positioning. Is the current positioning of your products and services vis-a-vis your competition or established players. Are your positioned as low-cost options, luxury offerings, or somewhere in the middle? The pricing of your products and services must be aligned with how they are positioned in the marketplace. Generally the higher the perceived quality of your products and services, the higher the price you can command from customers.

What is "normal?". So while you must research what is "normal" for your industry, for the region, or your competition, you certainly should not mimic what everyone else is doing. Most likely you are doing your startup to become the "new normal." In the SWOT analysis, you should collect data on what your competition is charging and how they are packaging their products/services. Existing players have done their research, and they have their reasons why they price things a certain way. You need to understand the "why" behind their pricing model

What are the goals for the business? What do you want to accomplish through the pricing of your products or services? Is profit maximization the goal? Alternatively, are you in a "land grab" situation where you want as many users as possible first and then gradually start monetizing later? As a general rule of thumb, it is not possible to maximize both short-term and long-term profitability with the same pricing model.

Are you trying to differentiate yourself from the competition? Unless you have an unassailable cost advantage from your "new" IP, you most likely don't want to differentiate mainly on price. Moreover, price differentiation does not always mean a lower price. If any of your competitors offer lower-priced products or services, you might want to differentiate yourself by focusing on the high value (and therefore higher price) of your products and services. In that case, you will need to communicate very clearly in your marketing message just how different (better) your products/services are.

There are a variety of pricing models you can choose from. For example here are some of the most common and relevant ones for startups (this is by no means an exhaustive list):

Cost-Plus Pricing. This is a traditional model that involves adding up all of your costs associated with marketing a product or delivering a service and adding a percentage on top for profit. Usually, the price is set at two to five times the product cost, but if your product is a commodity, the margin may be as small as ten percent. This model should not be used in an ultra-competitive situation as the trend over time will be toward an unsustainable low margin. The model works best when your startup's new technology gives you a tremendous cost advantage over others.

The "Freemium" Model. A popular model for Internet-based solutions where the basic services are free, but premium services are available for an additional fee. This model typically requires a significant investment to get to a critical mass of users and then requires hard work to differentiate and upsell premium services to users who started using the product first for free.

Ad Revenue Model. This is the most common model touted by Internet startups today, the so-called Facebook model, where the service is free, and the revenue comes from click-through advertising. It's great for customers, but not for startups, unless you have deep pockets. If you have real guts, try the Twitter model of no revenue, counting on the critical mass value from millions of customers.

Tiered or Volume Pricing. Mostly used in enterprise selling environments, where a single product may have one user or hundreds of thousands. In this scenario, a common approach is to price by user groups, or volume usage ranges. The tendency is to make this kind of pricing overly complicated, so you need consciously avoid doing so. This model is not used much in consumer offerings.

Value-Based Pricing. In this model, the price for your products and services are based on the perceived value to the customer rather than your cost. Also, the price to one customer type may be different than the price offered to another customer type. This pricing methodology works best for things that users absolutely need and can justify like health and medical solutions but not for "nice to have" products whose cost is hard for the user to justify.

Portfolio Pricing. This model is useful only if you have multiple products and services, each with a different cost and utility. The objective is to make a profit on the entire, with some products being "loss leaders" and some with high markups to bring the overall profit profile of the group of offerings. This can be a fairly sophisticated model with competition, customer lock-in, value delivered, and customer loyalty as critical factors for success.

Competitive Positioning. If your strategy focuses on putting a competitor out of business to quickly "own" the market, this pricing approach can work. Often used in the transportation and vacation industries, this model is basically pricing low in certain areas to drive competitors out, and high where competition is low. This pricing model used most often in established businesses, and startups should be wary of adopting it as competing on price alone is a good way to kill your startup quickly.

Feature Pricing. For products that have some intrinsic value to consumers even in only the most basic configurations or functionality, the practice of pricing the low-functionality version for a very low price, and then adding price increments for additional features can work well. Success with this model relies on designing the pricing/functionality options for good utility at many levels. This pricing model tends to be overly complicated so can be very costly to develop, test, document, and support.

Razor Blade Model. Like cheap printers with expensive ink cartridges, the base unit sold below cost, with the anticipation of ongoing revenue from expensive supplies. This is a model pioneered by large companies who have the luxury to wait for their profits to come in over time. The best versions of this model have excellent customer lockup and can bring massive long-term profits. Startups traditionally have avoided this model as it requires deep pockets to start, but with the recent trends towards larger funding rounds, this model is becoming more accessible to startups.

Free Product, Paid Services. With this model, the product is free, and the customers are charged for installation, customization, training or other services. While this can be an excellent model for getting a large customer base quickly, make no mistake, this is basically a service business where the product cost makes up a large part of your marketing cost.

Hourly Pricing. While law firms are most (in)famous for this model, it is not always selling people's time. Computing resources (e.g., CPUs in the cloud, machine translation, various types of high-end rendering, etc.) can also be sold this way. In this model, the customer is invoiced for all expenses and each hour or minute of work at a set hourly price depending on the services being offered.

Fixed Pricing. With this model, the startup charges the customer a set price for a service offered. For example, for developing a basic website, a company may charge a client a price of $5,000 to complete a project regardless of how many hours are expended or how many resources are involved. Of course with this price model to arrive at your average cost, you need to consider the complexity of services rendered and, on average, how much time and resources must be committed to each similar project. More so than with other models, without a true understanding of the costs, a business can lose money on fixed-price contracts.

Performance-Based Pricing. In this pricing model, the startup invoices the customer based on the performance of the product or service you deliver. Each price might need to be customized to each client and often will require a signed agreement between the startup and the client company. You should devote the time up front setting guidelines for performance-based pricing models and developing very clear metrics for achievement of the objectives. This model is sophisticated and most likely tailored to the customer's need so it is not scalable in the traditional sense, although it could be scalable within the client if they are big enough. Without the necessary execution experience, it is better not to attempt performance-based pricing models.

When choosing your pricing model, it is wise to test it out first. Even better if the test can be limited to one product or a specific subset of customers. If you are about to launch a new product or service, you may decide to test the new pricing model in conjunction with the launch. Be sure to keep customers abreast of changes you are making. Choose a group of core customers to test your pricing model--a focus group of sorts. A simple conversation with, or e-mail to, your customers explaining what the business is doing and why will it help to socialize the pricing model change and get buy-in and support. Your customers will tell you if the change is not acceptable. It is definitely better to know that before you make the change! Unless you are a brand-new business just opening your doors, you will likely need to socialize any significant changes to your pricing model before implementation.

Like everything else you do in your business, plan upfront and get input from those you trust and whose opinions you value. Understand what your customers want and be prepared to clearly delineate the benefits (to them) of the new pricing model you select for your business.

A Word about MVPs for Service Businesses

Throughout this chapter and book, I have been careful to refer not only to "product" but also mention services or "product/service" as your potential offering. The reality is that most product-centric businesses have some services component. Likewise many successful service businesses have "productized" their service offerings so the business itself can scale and serve more customers with minimal incremental effort.

Services businesses are good businesses and can provide a good income for the founders and other shareholders. However, until recently, if you asked a typical VC to fund your professional services company or consultancy, you would have the door slammed in your face. This is because the perception is that service businesses don't scale, and VC's typically only invest in businesses that have massive potential to scale.

The main reason service businesses don't scale is because they are based on manpower: to double your revenue, you need to double the hours worked. So unless there is unused capacity, that means doubling the size of your staff. Even then you can only expect to achieve 2x growth. Naturally, this level of scalability pales in comparison of that to the technology world, where revenue is most often based on a digital product—one where the marginal cost of making extra copies of that product is insignificant. Technology businesses can exponentially increase revenue without necessarily needing to increase manpower significantly. So when technology businesses talk about "scaling," they commonly mean aiming for 10X or even 100X growth.

Due to their need (as discussed in Chapter 7) VCs need to make 10x or more on their investments, they won't be interested if your startup doesn't scale, and most likely neither will the media or the general public. This is because the current version of the American dream isn't about steady, incremental growth— it's all about celebrity and riches. If you are just fine with a business scales incrementally, you might conclude that a services business—one that doesn't scale—could be right for you. Most likely with a services business, you will make money early and often, instead of working towards a future payday—which may never come. If your services business is positioned correctly, you can "earn while you learn" and start a highly scalable business on the back of that experience. I got started in entrepreneurship this way and with most of my subsequent startups found a way to earn while myself and the founding team learned more about the market we were interested in.

Net/net there is no need to overly influenced by the popular emphasis on scalability and success. Look at what you can do and what the people around you need. If you have skills they can use, sell them. Use those skills to get an inside look at other corporate and creative environments so you can learn from other people's mistakes before you have to learn from your own. When the time is right, and you want to build your scalable startup, do it on the foundation of a successful services business. You will find you have a stronger experience base and a more stable launchpad for your startup because of your consulting or other service business experience not in spite of it.

The Ultimate Validation Question: Is Your Startup Going from Zero to One or Not?

Most people copy what is already out there (i.e. they go from one to two). There is safety and comfort in it. Moreover, most people genuinely feel they can do it "better" or "faster" or "cheaper" than the other guy—because they are smarter of course! They modify it and may put a new spin on it, but in reality, they are leveraging someone else's hard work and market validation. This approach can, in many situations, turn into good business for the short term.

On the other hand, doing something entirely new or doing something in a radically new way (i.e. from zero to one) is the essence behind long-term, world-impacting business success. If you are setting out to do something incredible you need to ask yourself this question: "Are we building something completely new here?"

MOST PEOPLE, LARRY PAGE, OBSERVES, "TEND TO ASSUME THAT THINGS ARE IMPOSSIBLE, RATHER THAN STARTING FROM REAL-WORLD PHYSICS AND FIGURING OUT WHAT'S POSSIBLE." IN WIRED, STEVEN LEVY ELABORATED: THE WAY PAGE SEES IT, A TEN PERCENT IMPROVEMENT MEANS THAT YOU'RE DOING THE SAME THING AS EVERYBODY ELSE. YOU PROBABLY WON'T FAIL SPECTACULARLY, BUT YOU ARE GUARANTEED NOT TO SUCCEED WILDLY. THAT'S WHY PAGE EXPECTS GOOGLERS TO CREATE PRODUCTS AND SERVICES THAT ARE TEN TIMES BETTER THAN THE COMPETITION. THAT MEANS HE ISN'T SATISFIED WITH DISCOVERING A COUPLE OF HIDDEN EFFICIENCIES OR TWEAKING CODE TO ACHIEVE MODEST GAINS. THOUSAND-PERCENT IMPROVEMENT REQUIRES RETHINKING PROBLEMS, EXPLORING WHAT'S TECHNICALLY POSSIBLE AND HAVING FUN IN THE PROCESS. DOERR, JOHN. MEASURE WHAT MATTERS: HOW GOOGLE, BONO, AND THE GATES FOUNDATION ROCK THE WORLD WITH OKRS (PP. 195-197). PENGUIN PUBLISHING GROUP.

So be honest with yourself. If you are copying an existing business model, then at least own up to it and reconcile that with yourself. There is no shame inherent in this approach, and if you do execute better than the incumbents, you will reap the rewards. However, if you are doing something entirely new, "order of magnitude" new, "zero to one" new then strap yourself in as it will be a wild ride. Especially since no one understands what you want to do and will do nothing but doubt you and your crazy ideas for at least the first few years.

Tao Te Ching 道德经 Verse 55

He who is in harmony with the Tao is like a newborn child.

Its bones are soft, its muscles are weak,

but its grip is powerful.

It doesn't know about the union of male and female,

yet its penis can stand erect, so intense is its vital power.

It can scream its head off all day,

yet it never becomes hoarse,

so complete is its harmony.

The Master's power is like this.

He lets all things come and go effortlessly, without desire.

He never expects results; thus he is never disappointed.

He is never disappointed; thus his spirit never grows old.

6

THE PITCH DECK

THE PITCH DECK: YOUR COVENANT

Yes, you need a good pitch deck. A pitch deck overview tells the world who you are and what you intend to do. But no startup ever got funded on a pitch deck alone. The average VC spends less than 4 minutes looking at a pitch deck. Sending a pitch deck to a VC can only give them a reason to NOT invest in your company. While a good pitch deck may pique an investor's interest, a decision to invest will not be made just by seeing the pitch deck. Investors invest in people, not pitch decks. Spend some time crafting your pitch deck, show it to people, get good feedback and update it frequently. Personally, I almost never just send a pitch deck to an investor without a meeting first.

That said, the process of creating a pitch deck as a founding team is invaluable. You should treat it as a covenant. That tells the world—and yourselves—exactly what your startup was formed to do. The reality is at the outset; the founders will all have slightly (sometimes extremely) different goals and ideas of what your startup should be and also what it should become. By building a pitch deck together, you pull together your shared vision into one cohesive document that exists to pronounce exactly what you and your startup will do.

Learner's definition of COVENANT

[count]

1 *formal* : a formal and serious agreement or promise

I always encourage entrepreneurs to create a pitch deck really early. The entire process is invaluable for 1) helping you visualize what kind of company you want to become, and 2) helping you to find the holes in your strategy. These holes will appear as you write the presentation. The parts that are hard to write are hard because either you and your co-founding team have not thought them through carefully or they are beyond your current level of expertise. This is why the draft pitch deck should be reviewed, discussed, debated and changed and finally agreed upon by the founding team as a whole. While cathartic, the group process of creating a pitch deck can go a long way towards aligning your goals as a team and ensuring you all have a common vision of what the founding team is signing up to do.

Even if you never use the deck to pitch a venture capitalist, you must go through the process of creating a pitch deck as a way to attain internal alignment on goals and the outcomes you are spending the next several years of your life to achieve.

The best way to do a pitch deck is just to start writing it. However, before we discuss how to do that, let's discuss some key points. You should endeavor to create a pitch deck that:

- Is the embodiment of "less is more" and contains less text, more pictures (don't make it longer than ten slides)

- Is self-explanatory (so if someone looked at it without it being actually pitched to them they would still get the gist of it)

- Tells a story, visually

- Makes one strong point per page

- Would "wow" the folks at Sequoia Capital

Let's dive into why these points are important

Less text detail, more story

First and foremost realize that a pitch deck is a marketing document, it has to have a narrative and a storyline. Whoever is partaking of the pitch (either live or reading it) needs to be drawn into the story, enjoy it and be moved by the ending.

Too many decks are full of facts and figures but lack a cohesive narrative that makes them compelling. Dressing the deck up with beautiful visuals can help, but even if you do that and you don't "tell a story," you will be missing the opportunity to captivate your audience. Format-wise, instead of a novel or research paper, think more in terms of a short story, manga or comic book which can visually convey the narrative, emotions, plot that stirs the reader with a minimum of words and a short commitment of time and make them want more.

So when building your pitch and deck think first about the story you want to tell. You or your cofounder's story can be part of it, but it shouldn't be the entire story. More often than not it will be a story of a problem and a market that you have an idea of how to change. Lead the reader through that narrative and show them the promised land that awaits their funding. Before writing existed, humans communicated key morals, customs and history from generation to generation via stories and narratives. Music and dancing are first and foremost tools of this storytelling regime. The human mind is wired to remember and care about stories. Except for certain outlier situations or ultra-specific niche markets, focusing on telling the story is the best strategy.

Make it self-explanatory

The average pitch deck view time by a potential investor is three minutes and forty-four seconds according to a survey by DocSend of over 200 pitch decks. More often or not, the deck is viewed on a mobile phone. Even if you get face time with an investor, there is never any guarantee that you will have time to make any elaborate points. It is for these reasons that you should assume that the audience for your pitch will only devote 4 minutes to looking at it. The pitch deck needs to be done well enough to convey your key points on its own. That greatly impacts how and what you present in the deck. Keep this in mind when you are building it. If you feel your pitch strongly needs audio and visual accompaniment, then make a video. In that case, keep your video at around 2 and a half minutes in length. On platforms like Kickstarter and Indiegogo that help entrepreneurs attract investment purely online, the 2.5-minute length has been proven to be the sweet spot. Any longer and they will likely not watch through to the end. If they don't watch through to the end, they definitely will not be investing in your startup.

Tell a story, visually

For audience retention, you need to paint a picture, demo and discuss. That is the only way you will have a chance of getting your audience to get somewhere near 50% retention of the information you present. Most all of the data you present as text WILL BE FORGOTTEN. Before books, primitive humans remembered their history, culture, and customs by passing it down to their children in the form of stories acted out by people wearing costumes, dancing, singing, chanting and generally telling interesting stories. With all of our technological aides, human beings are still the same. The more audio/visual and the more participatory a pitch is, the better it will be remembered. And the better it is remembered, the more likely your startup is to be funded.

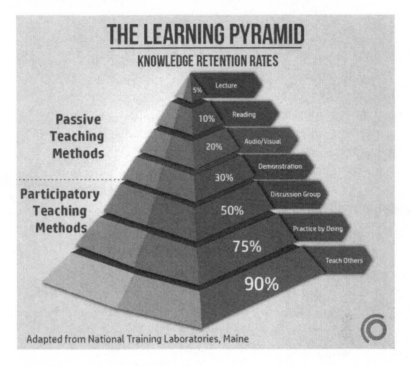

THE LEARNING PYRAMID
KNOWLEDGE RETENTION RATES

Passive Teaching Methods

Lecture — 5%
Reading — 10%
Audio/Visual — 20%

Participatory Teaching Methods

Demonstration — 30%
Discussion Group — 50%
Practice by Doing — 75%
Teach Others — 90%

Adapted from National Training Laboratories, Maine

Make one point per page

Don't fall into the powerpoint trap and have 3 to 5 bullet points you want to explain on every slide. I promise you will end up reading the slides and putting people to sleep. Other than the main point you want to make on the slide, anything written does not need to be said. And keep the writing to a minimum. Make your point using visuals and story elements as often as you can. Make it memorable, not a menu listing of features or a strategy script for you to read from. The deck is there for your audience, not you, it exists only to communicate salient points, and if you are giving the pitch live, it exists only to cue you to each new topic that you could explain with or without the slides since you live it and know it so well.

Imagine you are pitching to Sequoia Capital

Sequoia Capital is a venture capital firm founded by Don Valentine in 1972. The firm has offices in the US, China, India, and Israel. Sequoia has funded an extraordinary number of enormously successful companies including Google, Yahoo, Paypal, Electronic Arts, YouTube, NVIDIA, Cisco Systems, Oracle and Apple. Sequoia estimates that 10% of the NASDAQ's value is made up of firms they have funded. Unlike many of the other leading US-based VC firms, they are firmly established in China and not only play in the China market but are a bonafide leader there as well. Their position in both the US and China markets puts them at the top of my list. They also don't rest on their laurels and are incredibly active. Their actions speak louder than their words. When they invest, they invest big and are a fantastic enabler for the firms who receive investments from them. Therefore, I write all pitches as if I were pitching Sequoia. This ensures I am not sloppy, stay focused and build the best pitch deck I can build. Sequoia, in it's low-key, just the facts ma'am style, has made it very clear to entrepreneurs what they are interested in hearing from you. Their "guide to pitching" can be found on the Sequoia Capital website. I suggest you read through it both before and after you have built your pitch. Sequoia list ten things (reprinted below) to communicate to potential investors. I suggest you follow this advice on the whole as it is time, market and success-tested.

1. **Company purpose.** Start here: define your company in a single declarative sentence. This is harder than it looks. It's easy to get caught up

listing features instead of communicating your mission

2. **Problem.** Describe the pain of your customer. How is this addressed today and what are the shortcomings to current solutions.

3. **Solution.** Explain your eureka moment. Why is your value prop unique and compelling? Why will it endure? And where does it go from here?

4. **Why now?** The best companies almost always have a clear why now? Nature hates a vacuum— so why hasn't your solution been built before now?

5. **Market potential.** Identify your customer and your market. Some of the best companies invent their own markets.

6. **Competition / alternatives.** Who are your direct and indirect competitors? Show that you have a plan to win.

7. **Business model.** How do you intend to thrive?

8. **Team.** Tell me the story of your founders and key team members.

9. **Financials**. If you have any, please include.

10. **Vision.** If all goes well, what will you have built in five years?

While the "Sequoia 10" is as close to a perfect template there are certain areas I change up for each startup.

- Slide order: While I am not sure if the "Sequoia 10" is written in the order they think a founder should present the slides from the deck, I always change up the slide sequence to match the storyline, audience, strengths/weaknesses. Especially with early-stage startups, you will not have a "slam dunk" point to make on every slide category. While you need to be upfront and honest when discussing your weaknesses, it does not mean you need to put them on the first slide or declare them in 48 point font size. Don't fake, but don't hide either.

- Financials: I do not as a rule put very detailed financials into my pitch decks since once they are released into the wild, you have no control over who sees them or how they will be used/interpreted. Nonetheless, I always include core metrics to show potential investors the scalability of the business and the metrics that we as a founding team deem important to measure our success in achieving stated goals. There is nothing worse for your audience and your chances of getting funding than pasting an Excel spreadsheet full of numbers on a slide and calling it "the financials." Such discussions, if they ever even take place, should be done separately in close company.

- Business model: This is an area I tend to spend more time on rather than less. A serious investor will always want to understand your business model in depth, and a serious entrepreneur will always be able to articulate his or her startup's business model clearly and in varying levels of depth as required. Most new entrepreneurs don't spend near enough mental time and energy on this part.

While ten slides max is the goal, in reality, it seems most entrepreneurs have lots to write, and the average pitch deck has something like 19 or 20 slides. The folks at DocSend took a data set of a few thousand startups that use their platform and tracked how many pages were devoted on average to each of the "Sequoia 10" in the wild and which decks contained which pages.

Designing a Successful Seed Deck

Graphic courtesy of DocSend.

Jump in! Start making your pitch deck!

I have looked at thousands of pitches, and almost a hundred "how to" writings and I keep coming back to the "Sequoia 10" and the Airbnb pitch decks when I mentor people or build my own pitch decks. There are many other decks out there, and I suggest you have a look at 10 or 20 before your build your own to help fire your imagination and serve as a sort of inspirational template. In addition to looking at the "best hits" pitch decks of old, one thing I always do is find at least one to two pitches from a comparable or a relevant industry just to find out how similar or different they are. I also make it a point to find at least one reference pitch deck from a promising company that has been funded in the last three months. Things change fast in the world of startups, and you need to stay on top of the latest "pitching trends." Following are a few of the websites I use to find example pitches.

- The "Sequoia 10" template

- The original Airbnb deck and an editable template

- The original LinkedIn deck. It is a true classic

- Pitch deck consultant Alexander Jarvis has compiled a collection of 92 funded decks, templates and videos including the original YouTube deck and a seed stage pitch deck template and a massive pitch deck slide template gallery with 115 slides to choose from. I have never used his stuff but I included it here in case you need inspiration.

- Other resources.for designing one page overviews and pitch deck galleries.

So "What does a pitch deck look like and how do I get started?" you ask. Well, first you look at the "Sequoia 10" and build those 10 slides for your pitch deck. Think of the "storyline" as you are collecting the data and presenting it visually so the pitch deck can stand on its own. Do this before you look at all those other examples to get "inspiration." This will ensure you get your essence down in the "Sequoia 10" draft.

Once you have this done, go into your brainstorming mode and find tips, hints, and inspiration from 20 or so pitch decks that were successfully funded.

Then go back and refine your visuals, the narrative, the order and perhaps add a couple of slides. Note that depending on the nature of your startup and the market it serves and the maturity of the product offering, the pitch deck contents will change from the "Sequoia 10" and also naturally evolve over time. A good example of this is the Snapchat deck. While the core of the "Sequoia 10" remains, to emphasize the narrative and Snapchat's unique solution, some changes were made. The result was 14 slides as follows (13 excluding cover slide). No matter what you think of the Snapchat story, the reality is the company's pitch deck stands out as the most successful to date. Snap raised a total of $4,898,985,000 in funding over 13 rounds. So take some time to study the 5 billion dollar pitch deck yourself.

Anatomy of the Snapchat pitch deck

1. Cover Slide

2. Get to Know Us (Company Background)

3. Philosophy

4. Product Overview

5. Snap (Feature 1)

6. Story (Feature 2)

7. Chat/Here (Features 3 & 4)

8. Our Story (Feature 5)

9. How It Works (Using "Our Story")

10. Now It's Your Turn (Business Accounts)

11. What Do I Snap? (Marketing Tactics)

12. Get the Word Out (Promotion)

13. Examples (Early Adopters)

14. How to See Your Stats/Accounts to Check Out

OK, you can stop reading now! Go, go ahead and have a look for yourself (beware these sites will try to get you to subscribe to their paid services):

- Snapchat pitch deck: original version

- Snapchat pitch deck: updated version made into a template

Once you have created your pitch deck, just like your MVP you need to put it in front of people to get feedback so you can tweak it, re-order it, scrap it and re-write it or whatever you need to do until it is absolutely rock solid. The first people who should see it are friends and family. These are only so you can practice pitching it. You probably should disregard most of their feedback, but the repetition of giving the pitch 20 or 30 times will help YOU get better at pitching it. I then usually show it to 10 or so other successful entrepreneurs I know to get their input and feedback. The next step is to take it to VCs and Angels I already know or have worked with before. After these steps, I usually have a solid body of feedback and suggestions. I then do one major rewrite before talking to my investor "hit list." A hit list is about 100 companies whom you think are active, interested and inclined to invest in your sector. The reason I pull together a large list is so that I force myself to see which investors are active in which spaces. Whether it is your first money raise or you haven't raised since your last round our startup, things have likely changed in the market. Certain VCs may have raised new funds; others may be less active or not focused on the space your startup is in anymore. Creating a long list forces you to study up a bit before culling it down to the top 30. There are many ways to get lists of VCs, and you really will likely only visit the top 30 anyway before getting funded or rethinking your strategy. Having more investor meetings does not in any way correlate with getting more money

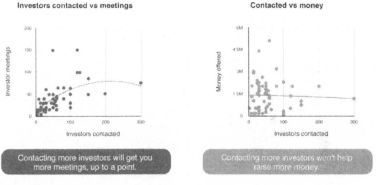

Strive for Quality, Not Quantity, of Investors

It's tempting to think that the more investors you contact, the better your chances of raising money. Unfortunately, this situation isn't the case. Certainly, the more investors you contact, the more meetings you'll get, up to a point. Note: in the data reported here, an entrepreneur could have multiple meetings with one investor, making it possible to have more meetings than investors contacted.

Contacting more investors will get you more meetings, but it won't necessarily get you more money. Focus on the quality of your connection to the investors you contact. In this graph, we compare the number of investors contacted and the amount of funding raised. There isn't much correlation, and if anything, the impression is a bit negative.

Investors contacted vs meetings

Contacted vs money

Contacting more investors will get you more meetings, up to a point.

Contacting more investors won't help raise more money.

Graphic courtesy of DocSend

If you do the necessary public events, pitch contests and get press write-ups, you will also have junior analysts at VC firms and Angels who watch the startup news contact you. With these, I tend to have a phone call to find out their real level of interest before meeting up. With investors who contact me first, I tend to avoid email back and forth sessions it is too impersonal and quickly becomes dry and forensic in nature. It always seems to devolve into "send me your financial projections" email requests prior to a meeting. To me, it simply makes no sense for someone you have never met to look through your pie in the sky financial projections for a startup you are just starting without ever meeting or hearing the pitch in person.

To Recap, Seven Key Takeaways

Fundraising for your startup can be an opaque and frustrating process when the future of your business is on the line. Keep these take aways in mind to maximize your chances of successfully raising a seed round.

More meetings does not equal more money. Focus on getting quality introductions to investors who are likely to be a fit. Quality over quantity.

Keep your deck to 20 pages or fewer. Each visit will only be 3m 44sec on average.

You'll likely need to contact 20-30 investors. But you won't need to contact hundreds.

Raising seed funding will take longer than you think. Don't start to despair until you've been at it for a few months.

Spend time on your deck. Specifically, make sure your team slide looks awesome. If you include a financial slide, which is optional, remember it'll be your most viewed.

Try to raise from a seed firm before you go to angels. Firms will give you more money in less time with fewer meetings.

Don't list your deal terms in your deck. Deliver them in person. The terms can vary by investor.

Graphic courtesy of DocSend

Make sure you program yourself to look forward to each investor meeting as an opportunity to learn—because that is exactly what it is! Getting funded is 50% hard work, 30% luck and 20% timing. What you learn in the process will be invaluable to you as a person and a startup founding team. At the end of the day, success in convincing investors is a first big step towards the success of the startup. And if you don't get any VC interest the first time around it doesn't mean you should necessarily give up. The next chapter covers the entire spectrum of funding options available to startups. VC funding is merely one of them.

Tao Te Ching 道德经 Verse 43

The gentlest thing in the world overcomes the hardest thing in the world.

That which has no substance enters where there is no space.

This shows the value of non-action.

Teaching without words, performing without actions: that is the Master's way.

7

THE FUNDING OPTIONS

THE FUNDING OPTIONS: WHAT ARE YOU WILLING TO GIVE UP?

There are lots of funding options out there. All have their pros and cons. Typically you don't need any money to start. However, you should think about what funding you might need and when or if you will need it. Where you get money to fund product development and growth is a decision that impacts almost every aspect of your startup--including your co-founder selection. Most first time founders feel that getting funding is the primary objective in the startup. It is not. First, you need to validate your idea and product. I have done "bootstrapped" startups which are funded by customer sales that have never taken outside funding. You don't need a VC's money to do a startup.

The following is a compendium of the different types of funding available to a startup. Familiarizing yourself with the entire universe of funding options will allow you to choose wisely and focus on what kind of funding is right for your startup. Remember there is an associated cost with each and every funding option. All of them involve a trade-off of some sort. Most involve trading equity in your startup for cash or someone's time.

PART 1: Pre-Traction Funding Sources (Phase -2 to 0)

Sweat Equity

The term originally came from the real estate world describing the effort an owner would put into a house or property to enable it to be sold for a higher price. The idea was that if the owner put his/her time into "fixing up" the property, the equity the owner had in a house could be increased because the property would be seen as more valuable in the eyes of potential buyers and then justify a higher resale value.

The concept as applied to the startup world is the time that the founders personally spend (uncompensated) in building the product, interfacing with customers, doing the marketing and promotion, etc., makes the startup itself intrinsically more valuable and therefore more worthy of investment from outside parties. Nearly all startups involve some form of sweat equity and the more value the founders are able to create through their efforts alone, the more indicative of the strength of the team and the business model to the initial investors.

Bootstrapping

Tall boots often have straps to help the wearer pull them on to their feet. The term originated in the 19th century where "to pull oneself up by one's bootstraps" was indicative of a seemingly impossible task. Today in the startup world "bootstrapping" is a prolonged version of the sweat equity approach where the founders can create significant value and revenues without any outside funding. Another way to categorize this is a "customer funded startup" where the founding team uses a combination of sweat equity efforts and revenues from early customers to fund early growth and product enhancements. Founding teams that are successful at bootstrapping are more often than not seen by potential investors as extremely resourceful.

Credit cards, personal loans, and lucky breaks

Credit cards and personal debt have a place in every startup. For every startup, I have ever created (and also for many ideas I have not acted on yet) one of the first activities you do as a founder is to buy your domain name for your startup using your credit card. Because this is done without any idea of when you will be able to get reimbursed, it is technically considered funding. I have always shared this early burden of paying for things like domain names, website tools, cloud services, etc., with my cofounders. The best way is just to keep them all in a spreadsheet shared in the cloud, so you know who spent what on what and who's turn it is to buy the next thing.

If you don't share the burden of paying for these things equally then, it will inevitably cause issues amongst the founding team as nobody likes to have too much personal credit risk. An important thing to discuss at the outset is how much "room" each founder has on their credit lines and how much personal debt they can stomach. Failure to discuss this type of personal spending can put unnecessary pressure on founder relationships and can eventually ruin not only the startup but also the relationship between the founders.

If it gets to the point where one or more of the founders (or founder's family members) need to give the startup personal loans then, by all means, do it but remember that equity has already been divided, and so loaning the company money has no impact on equity. Nor does giving the company a loan impart on that founder the right to suddenly take control of the startup's decision-making process just because he/she has more "skin in the game." While loaning the company money is a strong show of commitment, yes, but it does not give the "loaner" any specific rights, real or perceived. As with a loan you would get from a bank or other such institution it is important to have a clear idea of how the money is to be spent, how and when the money will be paid back (e.g., the company will pay back all the founder's credit card debts and the $50,000 loan from Bill's father when annual revenue reaches $500,000 or when the company bank balance stays over $200,000 in a given month). Make sure these terms agreed upon in writing by the founding team and fully documented, dated and signed. At the same time be aware that the terms are likely to change and therefore be diligent about updating the changes if the term needs to be extended, etc.)

While funding via credit cards and personal loans are pretty straightforward, you need to account for these and ensure there is a timeframe to pay them back. Also, there is another category that I call a "stroke of luck" Whether you get a local community small business grant or a prize for winning a pitch contest, any windfall that the company receives via its day to day business or the efforts of one or more of the co-founders should be allocated to the company and not any of the individual founders. For example, say a co-founder wins $5,000 in a startup pitch competition. That $5,000 windfall should be allocated to the company and agreement (in writing) about how it will be used should be made between all founders. Again failure to document the "use of funds" from this "stroke of luck" is just as important

Self-Funding

Investors typically prefer investing in people who are already investing in themselves and their startup. However, if you tell an investor you are "self-funding" it may make them nervous. It comes down to this. Are you self-funding because no one else will put money into your company? Why are you self-funding versus getting money from the variety of sources available to you that are outlined in this chapter?

Regarding self-funding if you are doing it post-MVP and post-revenue you are either on to something amazing, and you want to keep as much equity as you can, or more likely you are self-funding your dream project that doesn't have the proper fit-to-market. In both cases, you are need saying you don't require investment if you say you are "self-funding" so you should be clear with people you talk to about when (what stage/date) your company will indeed be looking for funding. So if you are self-funding tell potential investors your specific timeframe and doing it "until our MVP launches in August" or "until we sign our 1000th customer" or until we reach "1 million in revenue", etc.

Crowdfunding

Crowdfunding is an excellent way to raise money and generate enthusiasm for your product nearly all startup founders should seriously consider. The great thing is that these platforms allow you to test your value proposition and get experience with customers and fulfilling the product early in the lifecycle of your startup. Each platform has its niche, quirks and not all of them will be right for your startup but do be sure to investigate this avenue for fundraising.

- Kickstarter is the world's largest crowdfunding platform.

- Indiegogo is growing fast and in many ways a more flexible version of Kickstarter.

- Fundly has a social focus and is good for nonprofits.

- RocketHub lets you keep all the money you raise, even if you don't meet your goal.

- Fundable is aimed at small businesses who need money to expand.

- CircleUp is focused on consumer brands.

- StartEngine does equity crowdfunding and ICOs.

- Crowdfunder helps business owners find investors.

As an entrepreneur raising funds for projects, companies, and products, I have used both Kickstarter and Indiegogo. I find both platforms useful but with some important differences. For example, I find IndieGoGo more "international friendly" and flexible. IndieGoGo lets you choose whatever currency you like, where Kickstarter only supports a handful of currencies (currently Chinese RMB is not an option) and strictly ties the currency you use to the location of the bank account you choose to use.

That said, Kickstarter is more rigorous in ways that can be good for both the entrepreneur, artist or craftsperson as well as the people supporting them. Net/net both platforms have helped several hundred thousand people raise multiple billions of dollars without giving up any precious equity or control to venture capitalists and angel investors, all the while satisfying many millions of consumer's needs for innovative products and artwork.

Over the last couple of years, I have noticed that many smart entrepreneurs end up using both platforms. In practice, many experienced crowd funders do a Kickstarter first because the platform is more well known (e.g., better PR halo effect) and rigorous. That said, you do not want to fail on

Kickstarter! Because of it's "all or nothing" stance, on Kickstarter failure to reach your goal, means you get nothing, and your backers get nothing (their credit cards are not charged). Failure to fund on Kickstarter becomes part of your permanent entrepreneurial legacy--like a black mark on your startup credit history. However, once you are successful on Kickstarter, it is straightforward to transition to IndieGoGo and keep your campaign running for a longer period of time. Some entrepreneurs even leverage IndieGoGo as their main eCommerce go-to-market platform for the entire first year of their product or company's life.

Accelerators and Incubators

Accelerators and incubators exist to assist startups in successfully getting through the early phases and provide various services and infrastructure both soft (e.g., targeted advice and best practices) and hard (e.g., facilities and funding). The difference between accelerators and incubators is not well understood by many, and over time the lines between the two models has blurred.

Accelerators

Accelerators are all modeled in some way after the two early pioneers of this model TechStars (www.techstars.com) and Y Combinator (www.YCombinator.com) As of this writing; there are upwards of 3,000 accelerator programs worldwide with new ones opening on a daily basis. Since 2005 YCombinator has funded nearly 2,000 startups with a combined valuation of over $100 billion (much of that valuation coming from three companies). TechStars has also made a big impact on funding over 1500 companies for a combined valuation of $14 billion since 2006. It is safe to say that with the mainstream popularity of the startup model, starting accelerators has also become a growth business. While each accelerator program is different, the main focus is to help startups get a year or two worth of experience in a few intensive months. They have a fixed schedule for participation and have an application process. They also usually culminate in some form of demo day where the startups that have successfully completed the training are put on display for investors and the world to see. Accelerators typically invest a small amount of money (typically from $20,000 to $120,000) in companies in exchange for a single digit amount of equity (typically around 6-7%). Additionally, some offer additional financing of $ 100,000 or more in the form of a convertible note. The companies then go through a 60-90-day, intensive, on-site program where they fast track (i.e., Accelerate) their startups via help from the accelerators, mentors, and the surrounding startup communities. In China, I am a mentor for the largest Asia-based accelerator, China Accelerator.

In their typical straightforward, less-is-more style, YCombinator gives the essence of what they do in four sentences on their homepage:

Twice a year we invest a small amount of money ($120k) in a large number of startups. The startups move to Silicon Valley for three months, during which we work intensively with them to get the company into the best possible shape and refine their pitch to investors. Each cycle culminates in Demo Day when the startups present their companies to a carefully selected, invite-only audience. But YC doesn't end on Demo Day. We and the YC alumni network continue to help founders for the life of their company, and beyond. - YCombinator website home page

While I have never felt the need for one of my startups to participate in an Accelerator personally, I have spent several years a mentor at China Accelerator a top worldwide accelerator based in China. These top-notch programs like YCombinator and TechStars have been the place where some of the most successful startups like Airbnb, Dropbox, Stripe, Twitch, Uber, Twilio, Leanplum got started. However, as with anything, the trick is in scaling. YCombinator is a very Silicon Valley-centric organization and the program and as their class sizes increase from the original 6 to over 120 per term now, you need to weigh carefully if the 7% of equity for a $120,000 investment and the time you will spend on site is worth the once a week mentoring dinners, the demo day and support you will receive from the alumni network. Also at YCombinator these days most companies have to apply multiple times to get a slot, so that is another factor to consider. That said I know and like the people there and really find their open and straightforward style refreshing. TechStars, on the other hand, is extremely non-Silicon Valley-centric, based in Boulder, Colorado and has its "classes" themed to cities (NYC, Austin, Boston, Chicago, Seattle, London, etc.) or industries (Fitness: sponsored by Nike, Edutech: sponsored by Kaplan, Telco: sponsored by Sprint, etc.). With any other Accelerator that is not top tier like YCombinator and TechStars, you have to be even more discerning about what you are getting for the equity and time you put into the program. See who has graduated from their program and make sure what they are offering is really of value to you. These days there are more than a few accelerators that are run by failed entrepreneurs or small-time investors. Do your due diligence!

Incubators

By definition, an incubator is quite different from an accelerator. You can think of an incubator as a greenhouse which creates a somewhat protected environment for plants to grow. The prototypical incubator is Idealab which was started by Bill Gross in 1996. This pre-dates all the accelerators by the way.

We believe that entrepreneurship can unlock human potential and make the world a better place. We look for big problems in the world that have technology solutions and test many ideas in parallel. When one shows great promise, we recruit a great team, spin it off into a company, and help them grow a successful business. - idealab home page

In the early days of incubators before accelerators came along, the premise that if your startup gained traction while in the incubator there were funding opportunities available. However, over time the incubator landscape has devolved into spaces managed by any government, company, organization, real estate developer or wannabe entrepreneur who offers space and a set of perks for startups who are willing to set up shop on their premises. The problem with incubators is that by offering free or next to free space, they end up prolonging the life of startups that should have already died by now.

Incubators are a viable option when they offer some sort of geographical or vertical benefit. For example, an incubator run or sponsored by an automobile company may be a good fit if your startup plans to build products or services for the automotive vertical. A geographical advantage can be found if you are specializing in creating a new type of weatherproof outdoor gear and your incubator is located in a city near a mountain range where products can be quickly tested, etc.

Most incubators offer shared space in a co-working environment at a significantly reduced price compared to renting more traditional office space. Local government sponsored incubators may also offer tax incentives. When considering an incubator, you should look at the geographical, community, tax and vertical market benefits that can give you access to resources that will help your company be successful. Beware of incubators that try to push themselves as accelerators or startup creation factories. Again an incubator merely is an environment (like a greenhouse for plants) that will allow you to focus on your product. As opposed to Accelerators are more like industrial strength fertilizer for growth. Also, don't confuse incubators with co-working spaces like WeWork and the hundreds of other similar offerings which are straight up office real estate packaging plays.

Bank Loans and Micro-Loans

Full disclosure: I have zero personal experience raising money via small business loans or from non-profit lenders. With so many funding sources available, I have just not ever found myself ever even thinking about trying to secure a traditional loan for one of my startups. That said, as a startup founder, you may find this a viable way to raise a small amount of money. While I have always felt the time to apply for and get the loans were not in line with the time cost/benefit for the amount that can be raised, you may feel differently. In some countries other than the US, this is certainly more commonplace.

For Microloans of up to $10,000, you could consider sites like Kiva. Kiva is a non-profit that expands access to capital for entrepreneurs worldwide. To date, more than 2.5 million people have raised over $1 billion on Kiva. On Kiva, you sign up and get a few friends and family to invest in your business or activities, and then Kiva opens you up all their individual lenders who lend in micro amounts of $25 each. The lenders almost always get paid back (historical rate is 97%) but with no interest. The borrowers get all the money pledged (often right away), and Kiva does not charge any service fees, so the platform is extremely favorable to the borrowers.

I welcome any feedback on your experience. Just drop me a note on the website for this book

For those of you who want to have a look, a pretty comprehensive listing of (US-centric) non-profit lenders can be found at NerdWallet.

Also, the Silicon Valley Bank has made a name for itself serving the needs of startups and does loan money via convertible debt instruments if your startup meets their requirements. They have offices in the US, UK, Germany, Israel, and China:

Partnerships

My very first startup was a partnership, and since it worked very well for me, I have nothing but good things to say about starting a business this way—but only if you are starting the partnership with people you know well and have a good working relationship with. Partnerships are typically more suited to service or consulting type businesses but can be a very practical way to fund a startup if all parties have money to invest. Since partnerships by definition require each partner to put in his or her own money, this funding method is most often used by experienced entrepreneurs and people with liquid assets and a track record. Just be sure you have adequate legal documentation on how (and at what valuation) each partner can be bought out by others or outside investors if the situation requires. Some key points (from a decidedly US point of view) can be found on the following blog of the US Small Business Administration.

PART 2: Taking Fund from Accredited Investors (Phase 1-3)

Once you have shipped your MVP and you are in the marketplace validating your product/market fit you more than likely need investment from the people whose business it is to invest in startups.

Seed/Angel Funding: Angel Investors

The term "Angel " investor comes from the days when wealthy investors used to put up money to fund Broadway plays. They liked plays and had money to burn. It has been used in the startup scene to describe a specific type of very early stage investor since the late 1970's. The name Angel implies some sort of presence looking out for you like a guardian angel. Angel's invest early with a fair bit of passion for the project before more institutional investors would even give the startup a moment of consideration. Because they invest in the venture before the rest of the world begins even to believe you can be successful, they typically get a nice percentage of the company for a relatively small amount of money. Angel investors are typically wealthy individuals (many who have previously done startups themselves) that typically invest $100k or less in startups in exchange for equity or convertible debt. More than often they have experience or knowledge, the field your startup plays in. "Angels" typically invest for reasons beyond pure financial return. For some, it is a way to stay "involved in the startup scene" without actually starting and running a company. Others are in it to "give back" and find it a more intellectually stimulating way for them to invest money than more traditional means. Following is the US SEC rule 501 of Reg D definition of an accredited investor:

A natural person who has individual net worth, or joint net worth with the person's spouse that exceeds $1 million, excluding the value of the primary residence of such person.

While most bonafide angel investors in the US are accredited investors for tax purposes, angel investors can be more broadly interpreted to include friends, family, private or informal investors. Anyone who invests money at a very early stage to help the startup turn their ideas into products/services can be considered an Angel.

It pays to remember the one key difference between Angel investors and VCs. Angel investors invest their OWN money. He or she seriously wants to make a lot of money off of the startup you are building—a very personal and real way. On the other hand, the money the VC "person" you are pitching to invest normally isn't his or her own. It comes from investors. These investors typically represent the world's most wealthy people: sovereign wealth funds, family offices, pension funds, endowments, etc. Their portfolios are diversified and the investment in your company, should it be unsuccessful, will have minimal impact on the company. If you take on an angel investor, who has specific business acumen or industry connections to offer, make sure you leverage this fully. Unlike a VC which is investing other people's money, the Angel's personal money is at stake they'll be extremely motivated to help you succeed.

Finding an Angel is not hard. If your company puts out a press release or you get some early press coverage in the publications they monitor, a few will likely contact you. If you are out pitching your company in public, you will no doubt run into them at events. You may even want to seek them out by looking up someone whom you know or have heard about. The Angel investment community is the largest in the US, so the resources for finding investors are more prevalent there as well. There is an online tool called AngelList that can help with the matching process. Circle Up is focused on helping people find investors for consumer brands and the Angel Capital Association is also a good resource when looking for angel investment.

I use the word "matching" because working with Angel is more hands-on (some Angels are too hands-on) than working with a VC and the aspect of "fit" is of paramount importance. A good Angel will share your vision, be nearly as passionate about your company and success as the founders are and also be a good sounding board and mentor. Another reason you need to know Angel investors is that in more established venture investing communities like Silicon Valley, the "big name" VCs get all their deal flow from Angels and unless you have been invested in or at least recommended to them from an established Angel, they will not even look at your pitch. Net/net in most cases the Angel investment community is a good source of feedback and a great place to practice your pitch and get early investments before moving on to engaging with VCs. If you go the Angel route for your first funding, be sure to get your Angel to sign up to help you get additional funding from VCs and help with key introductions and advice.

Most founders get their seed round by successfully completing a few of the early-stage funding strategies above. For example, someone might bootstrap his or her way into an accelerator by generating a few sales to customers before the angel round. The businesses that angels invest in are typically less than three years old, have little or no "traction," and are still trying to find product/market fit. Net/net angels like to put a little money to get an oversized piece of a company just before it becomes VC fundable and begins to get real traction.

Bridge Round, a.k.a. Seed Plus

More often than not founders underestimate the amount of time and money it will take to reach the milestones they need to raise their next round of funding. When a seed stage startup runs out of money before it has enough traction to raise a Series A, or before hitting breakeven a bridge round is often necessary. The name is pretty, but it means going back to your original seed investors: angels, family, and friends to get enough money to serve as a "bridge" until you raise your next round. These existing investors are motivated to give as they are faced with losing their investment if they don't continue to fund the startup. At this time the founder must convince the bridge round investors that they are throwing good money at a bad startup idea. Similar to the startup founders, most Angels are optimists and are therefore predisposed to believe the startup will be successful. Also, ego considerations are often present. If the Angel doesn't fund the bridge round, then it says to the world that he or she must have been wrong about the startup and its prospects in the first place. As a founder, you should know that each existing investor will ask themselves, "what has changed since I made my original investment?" As long as their faith in the founder's ability to execute has not changed for the worse, they will fund the bridge. Any other excuse they give you is simply that, an excuse. Not funding you means they are basically writing off their investment to date in your startup. Of course, the terms of the bridge is important. If the seed round was at a $5 million valuation and the company has learned a ton and landed some customers, but the valuation has stayed the same, it follows that the original investors should put more money in. It's simply a better deal, and the company is more valuable now. However, if you as a founder have increased the valuation, you may find some investors saying to you "I'm going to pass based on valuation." Another possible scenario that you as a founder should be aware of is what is called a "down round" simply means you're going to reduce the value of the company, making the people who invested in the last round mark their investment down. When the investment environment is poor, as it was in 2000, 2001, and 2008, many startups experience down rounds. Often, founders get through these issues by offering bridge investors a bonus by improving their terms. There are a few ways to do this. One is a liquidation preference. Another option is issuing warrants. Either way, the investors will typically get two or three times the value of their cash in extra stock. So, if I bought 10,000 shares at $8 each, I might get another option—a warrant—to buy 10,000 shares for $0.01 each in the future. While these terms are frowned upon in Silicon Valley as they are considered predatory in the East Coast and in other countries where investors are traditionally more conservative, these types of "downside protections" are used more often.

One size does not fit all, and it is best always to raise a little more money than you think you will need to avoid spending

valuable time raising, justifying, documenting and closing
bridge funding.

Venture Capital

It is important for all founders to understand how VCs'
make their money. A VC firm manages a fund that they raised
from some of the worlds wealthiest individuals,
corporations, wealth management funds, pension funds,
endowments, family trusts and other people and places with
deep pockets.

The VCs' charge management fees in return for handling
the investment and disbursement of these funds. The
management fee is a percentage (typically between 1.5% and
2.5%) of the total amount of money committed to a fund.
These fees are taken annually, semiannually or quarterly and
pay for the operations of the VC firm, including all of the
salaries for the investing partners and their staff. For
example, if a venture capital firm raises a $ 100 million fund
with a 2% management fee, each year the firm will receive $
2 million in management fees. While this may seem like a lot
of money, it goes to pay all of the costs of the VC firm's
operations, including employees, partners, associates, rent,
high end travel to and from speaking engagements, events
and entrepreneur meetings, the latest in understated office
decor, office equipment and all the high end laptops, phones
and perhaps even company cars they need.

A VC fund needs a 3x return to achieve a "venture rate of
return" and be considered a good investment ($100 million
fund => 3x => $300 million return). In reality, only about 5%
of VC firms accomplish this. The other 95 percent are
somewhere between breaking even and losing money. So

those guys live on their management fees until they get their unicorn exit.

So keeping the numbers simple to give you a feeling for the business, assume a VC firm with a fund size of 100 million invests in 10 companies over ten years. First of all, in a normal scenario 8 of the ten will fail. But assume the venture partners are quite a savvy bunch and only five fail. Assuming the VC holds 20% equity in each firm, The first five will bring a big fat zero (5 x $0 = $0 return). The three companies that didn't fail but also didn't set the world on fire exit at $25 million each (3 x $7.5 million = 22.5 million) then one company exits at $250 million (1 x 50 million = 50 million) and one exits at $1 billion (1 x $200 million = $200 million). Even with those results, the return on the $100 million fund is $272.5 million or 9% shy of the "venture rate of return." And once the VC takes its 20% bonus for each exit event—in this case, $54 million dollars, the investors are basically just doubling their money over ten years. Which means it would be better off just left in a more stable interest-bearing instrument.

Basically what this says is that the VC game is a great racket—for the VCs. Not necessarily for their investors or the companies, they invest in. Of course, VCs need to invest somewhat regularly to show they are active but they only care about the companies that will end up with massive exits. Owning an asset can either cost money or make money. In the VC world "carry" refers to the cost or benefit of holding onto it.

WHAT DO YOU THINK THAT VC IS GOING TO SUGGEST WHEN FACED WITH A $50 MILLION EXIT THAT EARNS THEM ENOUGH MONEY TO PAY FOR, PROBABLY, TEN MONTHS OF FAMILY LIVING EXPENSES IN SILICON VALLEY? THEY ARE GOING TO SAY, "LET'S KEEP GOING. LET'S BUILD A

UNICORN!" THE VCs ALSO HAVE A BOARD SEAT, IN ALL LIKELIHOOD, AND WOULD PUSH HARD TO GET THE FOUNDERS TO SWING FOR THE FENCES—AND RIGHTFULLY SO. IF THE COMPANY BECOMES WORTH TWENTY TIMES MORE, THAT INDIVIDUAL VC IS GOING TO PULL DOWN TWENTY TIMES AS MUCH IN CARRY—$6 MILLION FOR EACH PARTNER! STARTUP FOUNDERS OFTEN SELL TOO EARLY, LEAVING MONEY ON THE TABLE. VCs OFTEN FORCE FOUNDERS TO HOLD OUT AND SWING FOR THE FENCES, RISKING BLOWING UP COMPANIES AND LOCKING IN GAINS. CALACANIS, JASON. ANGEL: HOW TO INVEST IN TECHNOLOGY STARTUPS—TIMELESS ADVICE FROM AN ANGEL INVESTOR WHO TURNED $100,000 INTO $100,000,000

Now that you know enough about the inner workings and motivations of a VC you should also know that in order to convince them to invest in your startup you need to prove your market is "big enough."

One of the most common reasons VCs pass on an investment is because the opportunity "is not big enough." For a VC to generate a fund-level return that is worthwhile, they need to invest in at least one company that has billions of dollars of value. In order to do that, most VCs decide that each one of their investments needs to have the potential to exit at or above that amount, all the while knowing that won't be the case for every single investment.

The issue is that in the early days, most really exciting companies seem "not big enough" to a lot of investors. This is because like most of the big unicorns you can think of, these startups are often going after markets that don't currently exist or seem like a niche opportunity (but in reality, are much bigger). This is the rub.

You also need to know that different types of VCs will be involved in different rounds and the rounds have different sizes and characteristics to them. While the scope of this book is not designed for entrepreneurs beyond Series A, let's go through the remaining funding one by one so that you will be familiar with the trajectory that all successful startups follow.

Seed Round

A seed round, if you have one prior to your Series A round will investors of smaller early stage funds join along with pre-existing Angel investments by typically invest $250k to $2 million in seed rounds. A seed round is the initial capital used when starting your business. You would raise these rounds in order to cover the expenses needed to find a product-market fit and a scalable business model. The reason this is called a seed round is that it occurs before product/market fit is achieved and the startup has little or no revenue.

The following "lettered" series A-E are for funding growth for a company that has a robust product or service offering and requires the capital to grow.

Series A

This is the stage that venture capital firms usually get involved. It is when startups have a strong MVP prototype or have already launched it to the marketplace. Series A funds are typically used to establish a product in the market and take the business to the next level or to help a company get the volume required to cross over into profitability. Series A rounds are usually between $2 and $15 million.

Previous statements notwithstanding, for startups that need serious capital to fund their growth, VCs are basically the only game in town. The Series A is the most important round for a startup because it marks the transition from a loose group of founders and seed investors to a formal company structure that has "governance." Proper governance means the formation of a board of directors which decides on key issues and holds debates regarding actions designed to increase valuation (share price) of the company. Before the Series A, founders typically answer to no one but themselves. There is no board, there are no board meetings, there are no board resolutions, and no one is focused on the stock price, because the focus is, as it should be, on trying to find product/market fit. Post Series A, the startup CEO will have to spend about 20 percent of their time "managing their board." This means, setting up a board meeting four to eight times a year. They will prepare a board deck, have a lawyer create resolutions around stock options for employees, etc. Essentially has a boss in the form of a board.

From Series A onwards, your angel investors who were cheering you on become passive owners and are usually not invited by VCs to join in the Series A and subsequent funding rounds. The "lead investor" on a Series A will normally decide who can and can not invest in the round.

Series B

Series B rounds become necessary when the startup has established itself but needs to expand its workforce, enter new markets, make strategic product investments. The VC funds that you approach may very well be different from your Series A VC's. You may need to talk to VCs who focus on later stage companies. These VCs typically invest $10 million or more in a Series B round. This Series B investment is about taking your startup past the development stage. At this point, the company is already making money and has revenue and an established growth rate. That makes it much easier to forecast your eventual market share and revenue and more risk-adverse, larger investors will likely become interested in the company. Series B rounds are for reaching profitability and to give you the ability to dominate your market.

Series C and beyond

Once you are a proven entity in the marketplace, ganks and large VC funds can invest anywhere from $10 million - 100 million+ in a Series C. If your company has shown consistent market penetration and profitability, these more risk adverse large players will invest tens to hundreds of millions to help your company obtain mass market adoption. Series C rounds can also be used to make strategic acqui-hires or acquisitions of companies that have technology or talent that your company needs.

Acquisition

In the startup world, there is much talk of "exit strategies" or "exiting," usually in reference to getting acquired by a bigger company. While an IPO can be considered an exit, the vast majority of startups "exit" via one of the following set of circumstances:

1.   The startup failed, and you're selling something of value, such as employee talent, patents, technology, etc. This is what selling the company "for parts" means. This is commonly known as an asset sale or talent acquisition (also see "acqui-hire below).

2.   You're making more than a couple of million in revenue per year, but you can't or don't want to grow the business anymore, so you want to cash in

by selling it. This typically happens when founders want to retire or start a completely new business with a better-expected growth trajectory.

3. A larger company is fighting for significant market share, and they are convinced that acquiring your startup could give them a market advantage. These are known as strategic acquisitions, and the price for your startup could be anywhere from hundreds of thousands to hundreds of millions of dollars or more.

An example of this would be when Oracle acquired Netsuite. Oracle could have spent time and money to create an app like Netsuite, but at the time, Netsuite was growing very quickly and was starting to make a dent in the small and medium business ERP/CRM market that Oracle was dominating in the Enterprise space.

Acqui-hire

An acqui-hire is when a larger company acquires a startup for its employees, not for the startup's product or service. Time to market considerations and scarcity of the right technical talent sometimes makes it cheaper for a large company to acquire a number of skilled employees by buying a smaller company. This kind of exit normally yields a much smaller return on investment for investors, as compared to an acquisition motivated by strategic or financial returns.

Initial Public Offering (IPO)

An IPO is when the shares of a company are sold on a public stock exchange thereby allowing anyone to invest in the business. IPO opening stock prices are usually set with the assistance of investment bankers who help sell the shares. Typically $100 million - $1 billion can be raised through IPOs.

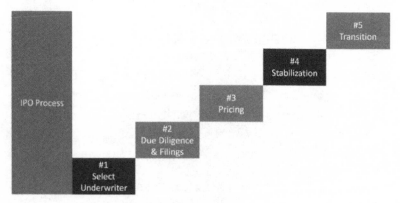

Step 1: the issuing company chooses an investment bank to advise the company on its IPO and to provide underwriting services.

Step 2: due diligence and regulatory filings. The investment bank (the underwriter) acts as a broker between the issuing company and the investing public to help the issuing company sell its initial offering of shares. The investment bank and the company collaborate to do the due diligence on the company's financial and business status as well as prepare and file various documents with the SEC (or other country's regulatory bodies.)

Step 3: pricing. After the SEC approves the IPO, the effective date is decided. On the day before the effective date, the issuing company and the underwriter decide the offer price (i.e., the price at which the issuing company will sell the shares) and the exact number of shares to be sold. Determining the offer price is important because it is the price at which the issuing company raises capital for itself.

Step 4: stabilization. After the stock issue has been brought to the market, the underwriter must provide analyst recommendations, after-market stabilization and create a market for the stock issued.

Step 5: transition to market competition. This final stage of the IPO process starts 25 days after the initial public offering, once the "quiet period" mandated by the SEC ends. From here on out, investors transition from relying on the mandated disclosures and prospectus to relying on the market forces for information regarding their shares. After the 25-day period expires, underwriters can provide estimates regarding the earning and valuation of the issuing company.

Most people think startup founders become incredibly wealthy post IPO. But that is only on paper. Consider the example of Nick Woodman, the founder of high-performance camera maker GoPro. The company went public in June of 2014. At the time of the IPO, his stock awards the year of the IPO were worth $74.6 million, but it's important to remember he did not cash those in right away. According to compensation experts, in the majority of cases, founder's stock and options at IPO time are less cash in the bank than they are incentive to stay and keep growing the company.

Founders with a substantial percentage ownership of stock tend to put some of it into the IPO pool to be sold and distributed directly to themselves. Lately, with the mega IPOs of Google, Facebook and Snapchat a lot of founders are doing things that ensure large payouts to themselves and also allow them to retain control post IPO.

Case in point. Evan Spiegel and Bobby Murphy, co-founders of the Snap, Inc. Which owns SnapChat, both sold 16 million shares in their IPO, bringing in about $272 million for each. Even after selling those shares, both co-founders own 210,970,819 shares, worth nearly $3.6 billion at the IPO price, and will together control more than 88% of voting power in the company. Investors who bought class A common stock in the IPO do not have voting rights.

Additionally, on the closing of the offering, Chief Executive Spiegel will receive a restricted stock unit award of 3% of all shares outstanding to be delivered quarterly over three years. This is worth an additional $637 million. Obviously, with these mega high profile IPOs, the founders have a lot of leeway to take money off the table at IPO time and retain control and large stock ownership post-IPO.

Salaries, Dividends, Profit Sharing and Private Placement (paying yourself)

Salaries and dividends are two ways to extract personal funds from your company. If you are a startup founder with a significant shareholding in the company, you should plan to explore both options. If some of your founders are full time and some part time, it makes more sense to set up a profit-sharing regime and pay more to those founders who are working full time, regardless of their shareholding percentages.

Salary: A fixed, regular payment, often paid monthly or bimonthly but normally expressed as an annual sum, made by a company to an employee. As a founder, you can set the salary to whatever you want as long as you have enough money in the bank to pay for it. For a startup the norm is to pay yourself well below the market price for your services and often the pay amongst a startup founding team is set to be the same amount per person.

Dividend: A set portion of your profits that are distributed regularly (monthly, quarterly or annually) on a proportional basis to all shareholders. If a startup makes $100k in profits per quarter, and you own 50% of the shares, then if you give out 20% of your profit in dividends then you would make $10k/quarter in dividends, and the other shareholders (typically investors) get the other $10k/quarter split evenly based on their shareholdings.

Profit Sharing: Similar to dividends but not divided proportionately based on shareholdings. Under profit sharing, profits are distributed in accordance with pre-set rules. More often than not the shareholders most directly responsible for generating the revenue are paid more than those who are not. This practice is common when some founders are working full time at the startup, and some are holding down other, day-jobs or have other commitments outside of the startup.

If the startup is not cashflow positive or a decision has been made to invest all revenue back into your business then the startup won't be paying out dividends because it will not have any net profits. That said you would pay salaries. The co-founder's salaries would be considered a part of the operating costs of the business.

In most cases, every startup founder will take a salary. Since salary is highly adjustable, for early-stage startups, there's no real incentive to set up dividends. As a founder, if you want to take home more money, you could simply increase your salary. If the startup's income and costs fluctuate quite widely, then you could create a profit-sharing system without calculating out dividends. As a dividend scheme is more formal and funds would be paid to all shareholders (including investors), dividends work better for larger startups with stable revenue growth. Net/net dividends are a way for all shareholders to take some of the money represented in the growing value of the company off the table prior to an exit. This is convenient as it allows investors to get some liquidity early without selling stock holdings in private transactions.

So it makes sense that the primary reason a startup will give out dividends in the first place is because investors prefer it. If an investor knows he/she can get a certain % of your profits in cash, it becomes a less risky investment since the investment can start showing returns earlier than if it was all dependent on an exit.

Private Placement: Selling stock in a private placement is a way of trading illiquid shares in your company for cash. Startup founders often find themselves in the situation where the majority of their assets are in company equity. To meet their personal financial needs, sometimes they will sell shares on private markets, like the NASDAQ Private Market.

However, as a founder, you need to be very careful when doing this. Unless your company is reporting very strong growth, selling shares can be a huge red flag to investors. This is because it sends a conflicting signal. For example, the general consensus from an investors point of view is that if you aren't willing to invest everything you have (money, time, resources) into your own company —why should anyone else invest?

It can also be a bad move for you to sell shares simply because you don't trust the majority shareholders in your company. For tech companies at a later stage, the board of directors will most likely be investors and the founders. If you and your co-founders start to reduce your equity in the company by selling shares to other board members or outside investors, the amount of founder control will decrease. Loss of control by the entire group of founders could bring all kinds of unintended repercussions.

For example, let's say two founders split 50% of a company. Employees have 5%, and investors have 45%. If one of the founders sells 15% of the company to the investors, then founder equity drops to 35% of the company. The investors now own 60% of the company and have majority control. With that level of control and if they are aligned on an issue—say bringing in an outside CEO—the investors have the votes to do it and the founders have no way to oppose the appointment. They wake up the next day and have a new CEO they don't know as their boss!

Summary

This chapter has covered all the main funding options available to startups. It is important to be aware of all of them as the vast majority of startups utilize multiple funding methods over the lifetime of the company. Each funding option has its pros and cons. The key thing is to balance your ownership and control with the funding you require. There is nothing worse than spending years of your life and countless sleep-deprived days but end up not really owning or having the ability to control the company you created.

Similarly, if you don't get enough funding at the right time, it could have an irreversible negative impact on your business growth and market adoption. Last but not least, if you go broke personally and end up destitute because you didn't take advantage of the funding opportunities out there then that perhaps is the saddest outcome of all. In all things, balance!

Tao Te Ching 道德经 Verse 44

Fame or integrity: which is more important?

Money or happiness: which is more valuable?

Success or failure: which is more destructive?

If you look to others for fulfillment, you will never truly be fulfilled.

If your happiness depends on money, you will never be happy with yourself.

Be content with what you have; rejoice in the way things are.

When you realize there is nothing lacking, the whole world belongs to you.

8

SPLITTING THE
EQUITY

EQUITY SPLITS: SHARING THE LOAD AND THE REWARDS

The ironic thing about choosing co-founder(s) is that from the moment you decide who will be the founding team, you then need to divide up equity in the company. This ends up being your startup's first big test of the management team must face a fundamental trade-off between efficiency and equality. Instead of fearing it, embrace it. Do it right from the beginning. Once done, don't fiddle with it or change it, ever. Do it once and then carve it in stone. While none of it means anything unless your company has an equity event (a sale or IPO), it can cause lots of issues amongst founders and ruin the company if done improperly or if constantly changed. If the co-founders know each other really well, they might be able to do this in 5 minutes. If not, a long discussion and a lot of things will need to be discussed. It all boils down to who will do what and what experience does each person bring to the team.

The reality is that there is no right or wrong way to divide equity. Moreover, splitting equity is particularly difficult if you have never done it before. Some people feel splitting equally is the fairest and easiest way—and it can be. However, as with life, doing things the "easy" way more often than not is a recipe for disaster. While the "fixed split" model is simpler and numerous formulas exist (some extremely complicated) for a more "dynamic models" that allow for equity splits to change over time. In practice, simple is best. Especially if you are working with "strangers," I find that an initial fixed split with vesting periods and a provision to deal with co-founders that leave early is the best solution. At the end of the day, the equity split discussion should happen once (early), and they should not be overly complicated or entirely contingent on future outcomes (as no one can predict them) lest you find the founding team continually focusing and bickering over them.

The real litmus test is to have a very frank discussion about who will be shouldering what responsibilities in the startup. Who is replaceable and who isn't. While it may not be the most comfortable discussion to have, for the health of your startup and to even give it a chance at surviving and becoming one of the startup success stories you are hoping it will be, you MUST have this conversation. In fact, depending on the situation, not splitting evenly could pay huge dividends in the end and enhance your relationship with your co-founder(s). So spend the time face to face discussing who is actually going to do what and who brings what to the table that will help the startup be successful faster. But do not spend any time on discussing who had the idea and who will put in how much money. In particular, money invested by founders should be handled completely separate from equity splits.

FOUNDER CHECKLIST

- ☐ NOT GOING TO CHANGE BUSINESS MODEL/STRATEGY
- ☐ NO PIVOTS THROUGHOUT LIFE OF THE VENTURE
- ☐ EVERYONE WILL BE SCALING/CONTRIBUTING AT HIGH LEVELS
- ☐ NO DOUBTS
- ☐ NO PERSONAL ISSUES

Graphic courtesy of Noam Wasserman and Thomas Hellmann.

The only time I would recommend a 50/50 (or otherwise perfectly equal) split is if you can honestly answer yes to the five questions above.

Let me say for the record I believe in equal or near equal equity splits. However, when you have more than two founders, or you have co-founders that have not worked together before, a more deliberate approach is required. Unless you have two founders who are known entities to each other and you also accurately predict the future, then it makes a whole lot of sense to go through a discussion and a process of logically getting to the right split.

In Hellmann and Wasserman's study "The first deal: The division of founder equity in new ventures" Management Science 2016, the data shows that 73% of startup teams split the equity within the first month. Most do it without much thought and split the equity pretty much equally. However, the result of the survey is that this ambiguity, in the beginning, foreshadows problems to come by not having the frank, often contentious discussions that need to happen in a startup to get goal and vision alignment. According to the study's authors, "Our central finding is that teams that split equity equally are less likely to raise funds from outside investors. The relationship appears not to be causal, but instead driven by selection effects across heterogeneous teams with varying degrees of inequality aversion." In layman's terms, the "quick handshake" approach to deciding equity just proves that the founding team is not prepared to have the kind of discussions that are ultimately incredibly important for the long-term success of the venture.

For example, in my first startup it was clear that I would be doing more heavy lifting (bringing in the customers, leveraging my existing clout in the markets we were targeting, negotiating the terms, managing expectations, being the face of the company, etc.) so I took the CEO role and suggested I take 60% of the equity and my co-founder (who was in charge of the technical side and basically the COO) took 40%. We discussed it face to face and unemotionally and matter-of-factly. The reality was that I was the person who was crucial to the market success of that startup. Then several years later I did another startup together with the same co-founder. A similar frank discussion made it clear that in this instance, He was the one who was irreplaceable. So, I suggested he take the CEO role and a slightly larger share. It just made sense. We had a strong working, and personal relationship and neither of us had an inflated sense of worth or ego. In each case, we just discussed the facts and made the right decision for the company we were starting. Both discussions took a matter of minutes to complete.

In the example above, our previous history of working together and the mutual trust we had built made the discussion simple. However, in subsequent startups, I learned a lot the hard way. The reason being, I had more co-founders than just one and also was co-founding companies with people I had only known for weeks or months, not years.

That said, history together is not a good thing when it comes to splitting equity amongst family members. People act differently at work than at home and more often than not, issues irrelevant to the business that originate from family history and hierarchy cause tremendous problems for the startup. The data shows that starting a startup with family members and dividing equity amongst them hinders the ability of the startup to reach its full potential. While some people have launched successful startups with family members, the overwhelming majority of evidence suggests this more often than not is a critical factor that causes businesses to fail. You need to take extra care and precautions if your co-founder is a family member.

Besides keeping the entire discussion emotionless, free of bargaining and logical, the best thing is to keep repeating the sentence, "What is the best thing for the company?" Of course, this question assumes that the co-founders share the same vision for the company. If you aren't there yet, get that done first (see Chapter 4). Also, the discussion needs to be predicated on the here and now. It needs to be viewed as a snapshot in time. There can be no allowing future possibilities to cloud the discussion. For example, "Yeah I have a full-time job now but when I quit and go full time with the startup things will sizzle." The separation of equity must be done on the here and now—the precise situation as it is the day the discussion takes place.

Beware of "tag along co-founders." I once started a company where one of the co-founders was an acquaintance who showed interest and asked to join the initial MVP discussions. My other co-founder and I misinterpreted this "willingness to jump on a plane" and join the discussion as a true passion for the project. In the end, that co-founder was the one who left mid-stream with many deliverables left undelivered.

As with anything, there are exceptions. Facebook's Mark Zuckerberg did equity splits the wrong way but survived it. His initial equity split with Eduardo Saverin was a source of unneeded conflict as the company grew. Mark's attempt to reclaim Eduardo's equity landed him in court. While Mark eventually prevailed, most startups would not have survived such a rancorous battle. So get it right the first time.

In many cases, you will need to bring on co-founders with whom you have little or no working history. In these cases, you need to be much more thorough and careful. Here's how to consider the following questions:

Do they deliver?

In a startup, the only thing that matters is the ability to deliver results. Lots of people talk a good game but don't actually deliver. Don't blindly trust their LinkedIn or resume. Ask people who have worked with the person before. Ask the person what exactly has he/she accomplished thus far in life and career. Ask questions that revolve around a number or are quantifiable some way. For example, what was the biggest deal you ever closed in terms of $ and impact to the company? How long did it take you? What were the two key issues you had to overcome to close the deal and how (specifically) did you overcome them? This line of questioning can easily be re-phrased to cover a specific technical deliverable as well. In many cases, I will give potential co-founders projects to complete to ensure they are a "get it done and on time" type of person. If you spend the time to understand what makes your potential co-founders tick, then you can do these things. I have asked engineers to build a better version of what we are doing in a vacuum before letting them come on as co-founders. I have also asked sales and marketing people to help us close deals before taking them on. If you feel uncomfortable asking people to do these things you are probably not cut out to be an entrepreneur. Go find a job instead.

Do they have opinions? Can they carry on a healthy debate?

You need to work with someone who doesn't just tell you what you want to hear. You may have the CEO title, but you won't be right all the time. Ideally, your co-founders should have strong opinions—justifiable and backed with logical reasoning—to balance things out when it comes to decision making. For key decisions, listening to all sides, then debating and deciding what is best for the company in an unbiased manner, is better than always deferring one person's opinion. In a startup, productive conflict and discussion is preferred and often required. Embrace it. It is not about "winning the argument," it is about doing what is best for the startup. In the end, it is essential that the debate and dialogue lead you to a better decision, regardless of who proposed it initially.

How you debate things as a founding team will be determined by your personalities and the culture you create. One extreme example is the two founders of preeminent Silicon Valley VC Andreessen Horowitz. Marc Andreessen and Ben Horowitz are known for how they use confrontation and tension to get to the best decision. Marc says the following about how he "torture tests" Ben's ideas:

"Whenever [Ben] brings in a deal, I just beat the -- out of it. I might think it's the best idea I've ever heard of, but I'll just trash the crap out of it and try to get everybody else to pile on. And then, at the end of it, if he's still pounding the table saying, 'No, no, this is the thing...' Then we say we're all in. We're all behind you... It's a "disagree

and commit" kind of culture. By the
way, he does the same thing to me. It's
the torture test."

Our human brains are great at pattern recognition, but they are also highly susceptible to innate decision biases we collect over time via our life experiences. So the founding team of a startup needs to have a culture that helps it get through these "biases." The concept of "having strong opinions that are weakly held" sounds like an oxymoron, yet it is a powerful process that is embodied in the Andreessen Horowitz case outlined above. Stanford University professor Paul Saffo developed the concept and is extremely useful in the startup scenario where many critical decisions need to be made early and without sufficient data. I particularly like it when you combine it with the "five why's" framework. If you can find a co-founder(s) with strong yet weakly held opinions, you can ensure that voicing great opinions will not be a problem in your company.

Richard Feynman
@ProfFeynman

We are trying to prove ourselves wrong as quickly as possible, because only in that way can we find progress!

10:07 PM - 21 Jun 2017

There are three reasons why the "Strong Opinions, Weakly Held" is a robust process for reaching the best decision or forecast when faced with complexity, uncertainty, and time pressure. This approach helps the team:

1. Leverage your team's collective wisdom

2. Overcome each team member's cognitive biases

3. Get to a quick decision based on the team's current, collective hypothesis

I strongly suggest you try this technique when discussion equity splits with your co-founders. How the discussion plays out will foreshadow your ability to work, interact and solve problems together as a startup team.

Do they have complementary skills?

To rapidly build and grow your startup, you need expertise in the areas you lack. If you come from a business background, you need someone with more technical knowledge. On the other hand, if you're tech-savvy, look for a co-founder with sales, marketing, and partner management skills.

This need for complementary skills also makes it easier when it comes time to divide responsibilities. Each co-founder can naturally fall into the roles they know and do best and bring their unique perspectives to overcoming challenges and creating solutions.

Bill Gross, the founder of Idealab and speaker for the Stanford Technology Venture Program, describes management team complementary skills in terms of four personality types. These four dominant manager personality types – entrepreneur, producer, administrator, and integrator -- complement one another and, in so doing, may be more important to a company's success than a business idea. For example, whereas the producer effectively manages the production, sale, and delivery of products, the entrepreneur provides the company vision. In turn, the administrator implements processes, procedures, and controls that ensure the company runs smoothly, and the integrator is the "people person" who assumes the negotiator or intermediary role for the team.

While this is somewhat of an oversimplification, it is relevant for understanding what each founder is required to bring to the table. If all your cofounders identify with the same "type" that is a sure recipe for disaster.

How committed are they? Will they do whatever is necessary to ensure success?

The only thing worse than starting a company all by yourself is to co-found one with a partner who is uncommitted. So take the time to make sure your co-founder is on the same page as you when it comes to commitment. If you're committed to working all day, every day of the week, but your potential co-founder only wants to work two hours on weekday evenings, problems will inevitably arise if you bring them with equal or near equal equity.

Communicate your expectations (goals, schedule, work hours, on-site/work from home) the beginning and update daily/weekly to ensure issues of commitment stay at a minimum. Also, remember, commitment isn't only shared in the short term! You and your co-founder(s) need to be on exactly the same page about how long you want to work on building the company, and what your exit strategy is. Because once the initial excitement of starting your new company wears off, it's crucial that your co-founders are still willing to commit for the long road ahead.

Many people can appear committed but in reality, are only biding time between their next paid project or job. This is why you need to ask them about their personal financial situation and their goals in the Maslow/Herzberg context (see Chapter 4). With people you don't have years of working side by side with, you need to ask probing questions. You need to dig deep into their psyche. Skip this step at your peril.

Net/net I am a fan of splitting as near to equally as the situation allows. That said, certain factors need to be considered, discussed and agreed to by all co-founders.

There is a great (not perfect) tool online that helps calculate suggested equity called the "Co-Founder Equity Calculator." If you are founding a company with people you don't know very well, the above Co-Founder Equity Calculator is useful to jumpstart the discussion on roles as it applies to equity allocation. However, avoid taking the results too literally. In my opinion, it is useful only as a starting point for further discussion. While I do recommend it for use as a reference only, but if it is your first startup, it makes sense to have each co-founder agree on the answers in a room together and see what the calculator comes up with.

Here is an actual result for a startup I was involved in. The names have been removed for privacy.

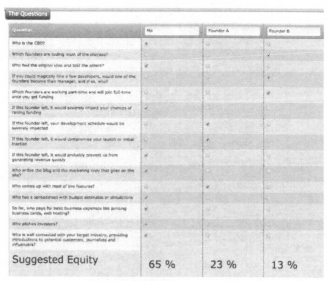

Graphic courtesy of foundrs.com

The outcome was that I took 50% and Founder A and Founder B and C took 25% each. Other factors were considered (mainly sweat equity and overall balance), and that is what we came up with. Everyone felt it was fair and it never was discussed again.

The siren song of sweat equity

To be clear, "sweat equity" is an over-used, much-abused and poorly-understood concept. I prefer Merriam-Webster's definition and the analysis below provided by Investing Answers.

Sweat equity is used to describe the non-financial investment that people contribute to the development of a project such as a start-up business.

Sweat equity is important to the successful start-up of a new venture, especially when cash is in short supply. However, it is important to value sweat equity carefully. In early stages, it is easy to overvalue it, offering stock in exchange for effort. However, over time, such trades can become very expensive and erode the equity available to follow-on investors. Sweat equity should be measured in terms of the long term value of the effort, the long term commitment of the participants, and the value-added by the participants to the overall goals of the venture.

In my opinion, sweat equity is too often overvalued in startups. Aren't all the founders massively investing their time and effort? Doing a lot of stuff and spending a lot of time is not an accurate measure of effectiveness anyway. Team focus on the results achieved and a determination to do things as efficiently as possible is much more important.

The Summary

No matter which method you choose or if your discussion ends up taking 5 minutes or 5 days, the key facts are as follows with regards to co-founders are as follows:

- Solo founders fail. Find a co-founder or two.

- Work with people you know. The best co-founder is someone you have already worked with

- If you need help from a stranger:

    o Do they get your vision?

    o Can they really add value?

    o Create an MVP together – can you spend a weekend in a room with a whiteboard and come out more excited than when you went in?

    o Try before you buy - can they build a piece of the solution or bring you a customer?

Full disclosure: Three Alternative Methodologies for Splitting Equity

The methods I have discussed above are those I have found effective in determining founder equity splits in my career. There are many other theories and techniques with regards to the process. For the sake of balance and your consideration, I present three of them below (NOTE: the names of each of the methods are mine, not those of the proponents):

Egalitarian Method: YCombinator is (in)famous for nearly always recommending equal equity splits amongst co-founders. Perhaps it is because their accelerator model forces the founders to come an live together under their tutelage for several months in Silicon Valley during the critical launch stage of the startup. The main benefit of this approach is that it is simple. However, unless you know your co-founders really well the risks outweigh the benefits. You can find this spelled out on the YCombinator blog.

Clock Puncher Method: For those of you with more of a bean counter or "charge by the hour" way of thinking, Mike Moyer of Slicing Pie is on a personal mission to promote these methodologies. I don't personally recommend these techniques as I feel they run contrary to the spirit of what it means to start a company that has a chance to make a significant impact on the world. To me, anything that feels like billing your time to the startup as justification for a percentage of equity is just plain wrong. However, there may be certain situations where these approaches might make some sense. The first case that comes to mind is that of a kind of a super solo entrepreneur who wants to distribute small portions of equity to the team of people who helped. The second is some type of crowdsourced or decentralized effort where equity can be leveraged to get people to contribute their time with the hope of something eventually coming from it. For more information, please buy Mike's book (which does have a lot of excellent information in it) or have a look at his website where he talks about the grunt fund calculator.

Algorithmic Method: There are some extremely detailed methods for getting down to your equity split based on extensive evaluations of data from a few thousand US startups. For the more academically oriented, math scholar amongst you I invite you to Google "The First Deal: The Division of Founder Equity in New Ventures" by Hellman and Wasserman and have a read. While I do not recommend these mathematics and data-intensive approaches, it may be useful to be aware of them in case you need to field questions from potential co-founders.

How to use "vesting" and the "cliffs" as a "Entrepreneurs Pre-Nup."

In your personal life, you get married "til death do us part" until you decide that is not workable and get a divorce. Yes, more people get divorced at least once than those that don't so like it or not the data is indisputable. Similarly, more startups fail than succeed. Prenuptial agreements (prenups) are not new at all, and their existence has been recorded since ancient Egyptian times. In the 15th century, the King of England Edward IV signed one with Eleanor Butler before their wedding.

So at this point, you're probably planning to authorize 10 million shares and issue several million shares to you and your cofounders. However you decide to split it up between you, there is one very important consideration: vesting periods. Vesting periods and cliffs are the "prenups of startups." Vesting in startups is different from that in established companies as employees of established companies vest "options to buy stock at a certain price" while founders earn their stock allocations over time. For the purposes of this book, we will focus on vesting as it applies to startups.

Founder Vesting

Vesting is a way for co-founding partners to protect themselves against the other partner if he or she chooses to walk away from the startup after a period of time. It can also be a way to protect the startup from non-contributing founders. At the founding, each co-founder gets an allocation of founder's stock. Getting a full allocation, in the beginning, helps avoid unnecessary capital gains and taxes. If one of the partners decides to (or is requested to,) leave after a period of time, and the company has taken on other investors (therefore establishing a value for the shares) the company will typically buy back that partner's equity in the business at the most recent established valuation.

Additionally, there's typically a cliff vesting period of one year, where if the founder walks away before a year, they receive nothing. The remainder of the vesting period is usually for four years.

If the company is acquired or purchased prior to the co-founding partners all being fully vested, there are two acceleration options.

Single Trigger Acceleration: If your company gets acquired, but you don't lose your job, you can accelerate your vesting by 25 to 100 percent.

Double Trigger Acceleration: This happens when your company gets acquired, and you lose your job as a result. This happens most typically with the sale of the company and the involuntary termination of the co-founder employee, usually within 9-18 months after closing,

The Importance of Vesting for Founders

At first, many founders are resistant to the idea of vesting. It might seem counter-intuitive since the chances of a co-founder leaving a successful business and an employee leaving a successful business are vastly different. It's common for employees to leave a startup before four years, but not for co-founders. However, because it's unlikely for a co-founder to leave, vesting becomes even more important.

You and your co-founders all agree on a vesting schedule for your co-founders stock. Recommended terms are:

Industry norm 4-year vesting schedule. Each founder's equity vests in 1/48 chunks every month for 48 months.

1-year cliff. If a co-founder leaves the company within the first year, they forfeit all their equity. However, the first 1/4 of your equity vests on the 1-year anniversary if you are still with the startup.

The reality is: startups are stressful and time-consuming, co-founders leave. The last thing you want is to fall out with a co-founder a month after the company is formed and have them walk away with half of the company. An overwhelmingly large number of company blowups are the result of co-founder fights. Protect yourself. See Cooley Go's Founder Basics for more on this topic. They also have some useful legal document templates on the site.

Note: The legal and tax treatment aspects of vesting varies significantly from country to country. Get counsel from legal and tax professionals as required!

Each startup I have co-founded or mentored has ended up having a different way of splitting the equity: some do it up-front, others wait to get to know each other; some go through a careful negotiation process, others are quick to shake hands and get on with the business of starting up the company. More importantly, some divide the equity equally amongst all founders; others conclude that the fair outcome is an uneven split that reflects differences among founders. I find that having an honest discussion about how the equity should be divided ends up being one of the most productive (sometimes cathartic) discussions between co-founders in the early stage of the startup. You should not avoid the issue, instead, deal with it head-on. Good luck and whatever you eventually decide, stick with it, honor your decision and don't revisit it again. That way you can focus 100% on making the startup a success and don't spend any more time counting your chickens before they have hatched.

Tao Te Ching 道德经 Verse 14

Look, and it can't be seen.

Listen, and it can't be heard.

Reach, and it can't be grasped.

Above, it isn't bright.

Below, it isn't dark.

Seamless, unnamable, it returns to the realm of nothing.

Form that includes all forms, image without an image,

subtle, beyond all conception.

Approach it and there is no beginning; follow it and

there is no end.

You can't know it, but you can be it, at ease in your own

life.

Just realize where you come from: this is the essence of

wisdom.

9

THE VALUATION

Valuation: Is in the Eyes of the Beholder

How much is your startup worth? There are no real rules or guidelines for setting the value of a startup company, but coming up with a valuation is absolutely necessary if you plan to accept money from an investor. This is the part of the startup process where the startup founder(s) and the investor(s) interests are diametrically opposed. The investor wants the most shares of your company for the lowest price, and the founder(s) want to give up the fewest shares for the highest price. Getting investors to believe in you and your ability to deliver is key. There are no rules or formulas for doing this equitably. It is a pure negotiation. The purpose of this chapter is to take you through what you need to know to understand how investors think about valuation and how you come up with and more importantly, justify your valuation.

Whether you like it or not, if an angel or VC is even mildly interested they will ask about your valuation. Usually, they ask this question to get to a quick yes or no answer in their own minds. They likely have preconceived notions of what valuations should be in your sector and what they have invested in previously. They ask you this question to check to see if you are currently undervaluing or overvaluing your company (according to their subjective criteria). If the number you provide them is too high, they will likely feel you are disconnected from reality. If the number you provide is too low, they may begin to wonder if it is something worth investing in at all seeing that you don't value it very highly. If you are unsure of your valuation or cannot defend it, then it merely shows them your lack of experience and sophistication. In any event, you WILL be asked this question by nearly every investor you meet at the very first meeting.

Therefore, it makes much sense to do some serious thinking about it before you start talking to people.

So when do you need to define a valuation for your startup? Usually not until you begin to think about seeking outside money from either an Angel or VC.

So how do you come up with a valuation? The reality is that while there are some guidelines for valuations in specific industries and markets based on past transactions, in most cases if you are genuinely doing "something new" none of these will be directly relevant. Also unless you have revenue and operating history of at least a year or two, then financial methods (EBITDA multiples or revenue multiples based on industry comparables) will only be useful in a hypothetical sense.

At the early stage, the value of the company is pretty much zero, but the valuation has to be a lot higher than that. Because to attract investors you need to show the company's potential for growth. Valuation does not happen until someone pays something for shares of your company. For example, in a fairly typical seed investment of around $100,000 for 10% of your company, the pre-money valuation will be $ 1 million. This does not necessarily mean that your company is worth $1 million now. It simply says that your seed investor(s) see enough growth potential to value it as such. You most likely could not sell it for that amount. So the critical point is that valuation at the early stages is a lot about the growth potential (believing in the team, product, and future revenues, etc.) as opposed to the current value.

As the true success of a startup doesn't rely on it receiving a high valuation often it is better not to demand a high valuation. If you get a high valuation for your seed round, you need a higher one for the next funding round, meaning that a lot of growth is necessary between rounds. You need to be aggressive yet pace yourself. The startup journey is much more like a marathon than a sprint in this regard. The way you set your valuation should be in line with your pace as a company.

A good general rule to follow is that within 18 months a promising startup will need to show that it grew ten times (in revenue, customers or whatever the key metric is). This type of growth is usually achieved with one of the two following strategies.

Land Grab – endeavor to raise as much money as possible at the highest valuation possible, spending that money to drive rapid growth as quickly as possible. If successful, a startup will have a much bigger valuation in the next funding round and often, the 'Seed' round will pay for itself.

Pay As You Go – a startup raises only the amount of money that it absolutely needs, spending as little as possible while driving to build a steady revenue base for growth.

The main difference is that with the Land Grab you are basically buying your way to a market position and/or prime the demand pump, while with the Pay As You Go strategy you will focus on executing extremely well with a little funds as possible to make your early customers happy and want to refer you to others.

Obviously, the land grab approach can boost you into the stratosphere, but a poorly executed land grab approach take you to a place 18 months later with a lot of money spent but not much to show for it. You will no doubt grow slower on the "pay as you go" plan but if you are tweaking and refining your product and value proposition along the way, it could be time well spent (without spending all the money.

So valuation for a startup in the early stage is best looked at from a bottoms-up perspective. How much cash will you need to run the company—and achieve your already finely-tuned goals— in the first year? Start there. Come up with a number. Then think seriously about the amount of revenue you can generate in that first year from your MVP. Think about your best case, likely case and worst case scenarios. You worst case scenario will likely be zero or close to it. Your likely case will be what is possible based on what you can already visualize then cut in half. Your best case scenario is the one where everything you can see now becomes revenue, and if certain opportunities don't materialize, new ones will come up to take their place.

Your worst case scenario for first-year revenue minus your expected first-year expenses equals your Seed Capital requirement. Refer to Chapter 7 for more information on funding sources. So seed capital is the initial amount of money you need to start the business. If you don't get your seed capital from founders or family, then you may need to go to an Angel investor. Investing at the seed stage of a startup is a risky proposition, and typically VCs do not get involved.

According to Marc Andreessen of the VC firm Andreessen and Horowitz, the VC game is one of "extreme exceptions" or outliers. Every year:

- Around 4000 companies come into the marketplace that are "fundable."

- Approximately 200 of these get funded by "top tier" VC firms

- Of those 15 get to 100M in revenue eventually

- These 15 generate 97% of the returns for that year's cohort

Marc also says his firm "Invests in strength versus lack of weakness. The outliers that are the companies that will win big almost always have extreme weaknesses as well as strengths." So the strengths of the team and the solution is the main reason that people will invest in you. Therefore when you value the company, focus on valuing your strengths.

So in the early stages valuation, the main points are valuing the strengths of the team (experience, technical or other skill sets and ability to execute as a team) and valuing the mid-term value of the opportunity. It is not a number-crunching exercise. It is a negotiation followed by an agreement that balances the upside and loss of control risk the entrepreneur faces and the downside risk the investor is shouldering.

The second key thing to understand is as a founder your equity will go down as you take on investors and in the process justify more substantial investments.

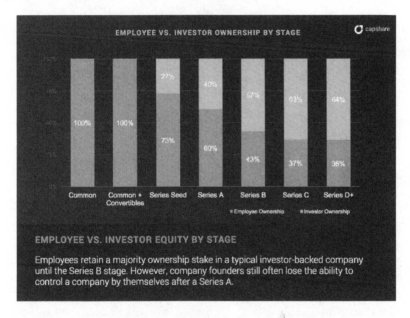

EMPLOYEE VS. INVESTOR EQUITY BY STAGE

Employees retain a majority ownership stake in a typical investor-backed company until the Series B stage. However, company founders still often lose the ability to control a company by themselves after a Series A.

Basic Valuation Terminology. The following terms are what you need to be familiar with to have the valuation discussion:

Equity. The term equity equates with the ownership of the startup— who owns how much. Usually, the founders own 100% equity of the startup at formation, then over time and the subsequent rounds give up ownership blocks to outside investors in exchange for cash investments. Smaller pieces of equity are also usually given to key employees in the form of stock options as additional compensation for their contributions to the startup's efforts. If a startup gets acquired by a larger company, the percentage of equity ownership determines how the proceeds from the exit get divided.

Seed Round. In common usage, a seed round can be any investment in a startup used to start the company and create its first products or services. Money coming from the founders themselves, friends and family, or other support associated with the entrepreneurs that are starting the company can all qualify as a seed round.

Series. Post seed (or Angel) rounds are grouped as "series." For example, Series A is the first Venture Capital level investment round. Future investments from institutional investors follow the same pattern, Series B, Series C, and so on. More often than not, there are one or more specific "uses of funds" for each round. For example, product enhancements, sales and marketing ramp up, international expansion, etc.

Investment Round. The process of raising money for your startup is called a round or a raise. No matter what stage you are in the money-raising process (just starting or just received the funds transfer in your company's bank account) each round is given a name that the industry understands, such as Seed round or Series A, B, C, or D round.

Pre-money Valuation. This is the value placed on a startup before an investment round. This pre-money valuation is the primary point of negotiation between founders and equity investors.

Post-money Valuation. This is the value of the startup after the investment round. It is the investment amount + the pre-money valuation = the post-money valuation.

Founder Dilution. The percent amount of ownership given up by startup founders, e.g., " the founders agree to accept a 20% dilution in exchange for a $ 250,000 angel investment."

Investor Dilution. If there are other existing investors in the startup, then founders are not the only stakeholders that give up equity as new investors show up. Existing investors are often required to withstand a reduction in their ownership percentage in the startup. In the case of a startup that raises multiple rounds of equity investment, early investors will need to give up some ownership to new investors. For this reason, investors often invest in preferred shares that contain anti-dilution rights in an attempt to limit their exposure to future dilution. Dilution is a key consideration for both the founders and investors. For more information on dilution, search Capshare has leveraged the over 10,000 companies in their database to analyze the equity ownership trends amongst private companies. For reference purposes, the graphic below can serve as a benchmark to track equity % shifts between the employees (founders, mostly) and the investors of a "typical" startup.

So how does the valuation of a startup work in reality? Let's go through a hypothetical yet detailed example.

Establishing Anchors

During standard decision making, individuals tend to overly rely, on a specific piece of information or a particular value called an "anchor" and then when factoring in possibilities in deciding to adjust to those values to account for other elements of the circumstance.

Usually, once the anchor is set, there is a bias toward that particular value or factor over and above all other items whether logical or not.

> *Anchoring is a term used in psychology to describe the common human tendency to rely too heavily on, or "anchor," on one trait or piece of information when making decisions. - Science Daily*

To successfully negotiate your valuation you need to create some sort of cognitive bias in the form of an anchor. The most often-utilized way to do this is to start with your bottoms up cash requirements. As previously mentioned you need to figure out how much money you need to grow the business to a point where you will show significant growth and therefore be able to raise the next round of investment. To keep the numbers round and simple, let's say that is $100,000, to last you 12 months. Starting like this, your investor will NOT be inclined to negotiate the amount down because that is the amount you have stated as the minimum amount you need to grow to get the business to the next stage. And getting the company to its next stage of growth and investment is precisely what your investor wants.

So if your investor declines at this stage, it is because he/she is not convinced of the idea, opportunity or some combination thereof. Or (less likely) he/she does not have the money. In this way, you can "anchor" the investment amount and focus the negotiation on only one factor: the amount of the company you would be willing to give up for that price.

Now with the amount of money you know you need no longer an issue of contention, you need to decide how much of the company you are willing to part with. Let's assume it won't be more than 50% because that will leave the founder(s) with little incentive to work hard. And 40% would be difficult as well because that will leave very little equity for investors in your next round. Now 30% might be reasonable if you were getting a large amount of seed money. However, in this case, since you are looking for only a relatively small amount ($100, 000), you will more likely spend the bulk of your time negotiating in a range from 5% to 20% of the company, depending on how well you can justify your valuation.

Once you get to this point, the $100,000 is fixed, and 5%-20% equity is also fixed. So that puts the (pre-money) valuation somewhere between $500,000 (if you give away 20% of the company for $100,000) and $2 Million (if you give away 5% of the company for $100,000).

Top three valuation factors

Once these "anchor points" are set it really comes down to 3 factors:

1. Comparables: how other investors have valued similar companies. List them from lowest to highest

and least similar to most similar to establish a range.

2.   Founder(s) Track Record: what each founder brings to the table in regards to previous execution experience. Do any founders have previous exits, specific technical or market experience, etc.?

3.   Market/Product Potential: How well you can convince the investor that you really will grow fast. This will depend on the size of the target market, the number, and nature of potential competitors, regulatory factors, etc.

Other key factors

Reputation. Based on past success and the way the entrepreneur is viewed in the marketplace, people like Reid Hoffman, Mark Zuckerberg, or Jeff Bezos would warrant a high valuation no matter what his next idea is. In general, Entrepreneurs with prior exits also tend to get higher valuations. That said, based on their vision and passion for the project, some people receive significant funding without traction or prior successes.

Revenues. Usually, revenues are more important for B-to-B startups than consumer startups. Having significant upward-trending revenue make the company easier to value as it makes projecting future revenue trends easier. However, for consumer startups having a revenue might lower the valuation in the early stages of the startup's life. Though it may seem incongruous, it actually makes sense. If you are charging users, your company will grow slower. Slower growth means less money over a longer period of time. That equals a lower valuation in the short term. This is because startups are not only about making money and being profitable, it is about growing very fast while making money. If the growth is not fast, then the valuation will be looked through the lens of a small business, not a startup.

Intellectual Property (IP). If the startup or its founders hold significant IP (patents, trademarks, trade secrets or know-how), this can be a factor in valuation. Especially if these IP advantages are such that they are not easily copied or reverse-engineered by competitors.

Distribution Channel: Regardless of whether your product is in the very early stages, if you have already secured a distribution channel for it then you could perhaps justify a higher valuation. For example, if an established company has already decided to distribute your product, and you have a contract that stipulates that you should be able to justify a higher valuation based on the expected sales revenue from the partner.

Heat Factor: In every year there are a few areas that can be considered "hot." At the time of this writing, anything that has an Artificial Intelligence (AI) angle to it is considered "hot" for example. Investors are particularly susceptible to the herding instinct and often invest in the same kinds of things in a given year. If something is hot, they may pay a premium for the chance to play and beef up their portfolio with the latest hot thing. This is one of those things you just need to be aware of and leverage if possible; it should never be the foundation of your valuation strategy, though.

New entrepreneurs tend to either undervalue or overvalue their startup in the early phases. The best thing to do is set a range for the money you need. That will give you a feel for your valuation range. That is the range you will need to justify. As previously stated if you need $100,000 and are willing to give up 10% for it then your valuation is $1 million. It all comes down to these two things: You know how much you need. That number is fixed, but if you are wavering around how much equity you give up for it, then the decision rests on your burn rate and your runway (how much time you have left before you run out of money completely). If you don't like the investor or the terms, then think about what you can do to bring in cash from customers to extend your runway until you do find an investor and terms you can live with.

Is a high valuation important?

Not necessarily. If you get a high valuation for your seed round, for the next round you need an even higher valuation. That means you need to grow quite a lot between the two rounds.

A general rule of thumb would be that within 18 months you need to show that the business grew by a factor of ten. If you don't, you more than likely will have to raise a "down round," where you are forced to raise money at a lower valuation than your previous round. Unless macroeconomic factors make raising difficult for all startups, having a down round creates the impression that the startup might be running out of gas.

Does the actual valuation amount really matter?

Consider two often-cited scenarios – Instagram vs. Dropbox. Both Dropbox and Instagram started modestly from one visionary founder. Both of them ended up being valued over $1 Billion. However, they started with very different valuations. Kevin Systrom received $500,000 from

Baseline Ventures in exchange for about 20% of Brbn (the predecessor of Instagram). So Instagram's initial valuation was $2.5 million. Drew Houston enrolled in the Y-Combinator acceleration program, where he received approximately $20,000 in exchange for 5% of Dropbox. That resulted in a valuation $400,000 (pre-money).

So why did the valuations end up so different? And, perhaps more importantly, did it even matter in the end? You be the judge. When all is said and done, the main thing is to get a decent valuation and retain control of the company.

The investor's perspective

As you consider how much equity to give up for how much money in this very personal labor of love that is your startup, it makes a lot of sense to understand what the typical investor considers important.

Exit potential. Investors are looking for the next unicorn. But they are also realistic and know that a more likely exit scenario does not involve an IPO. More often than not, it will be an acquisition by a larger player in the same general space. The investor will be thinking how much can this company sell for several years from now.

Total money required. The next thing an investor will consider is how much total money it will take you to grow the startup to the point that someone will buy it for say $1 billion. Yes, they want to get a feel for how much they might become diluted if they don't keep investing pro rata and the amount of funds your startup will need to raise over its life cycle. As $1 billion is exactly what Instagram sold to Facebook for, let's look at that scenario in detail. As a startup, Instagram raised a total of $56 million in funding. So bought by Facebook at $1 billion – $56= $ 940 million—that is how much value the company created. It's fair to assume that any debts were deducted and the operational costs have been taken out as well. So everyone involved in Instagram collectively made around $940 million on the day Facebook bought them. NOTE: although the purchase price was $1 billion, the final price was around $715 million due to a subsequent decline in the value of Facebook's stock. So the "best deal ever" in recent tech history was even a better deal for Facebook than when first reported. Remember this and tell your lawyers when someone offers you $1 billion in stock to buy your company someday!

Dilution over time. Continuing with the Instagram example, the investor will figure out what percentage of that she owns. Let's look at the investment Baseline Ventures made on Instagram which was $500,000 for 20% of the company. Assuming fairly normal dilution in the following rounds as Instagram kept raising money up to the $56 million amount, Baseline Ventures gets diluted to 4%. 4% of $940 million is $37.6 Million. So $37.6 Million is the absolute best case scenario for Baseline Ventures' $500,000 invested. That is 75.2 times return on money invested. Obviously an incredibly successful investment! But say in your case your startup turns out not to be an Instagram class success story. If your investor thinks she can make 10X on your startup that is still an excellent return in VC terms. So if after the original investment of 500,000 you raised $3 Million in exchange for 4% – that would give the original investor a 10X returns, ten times their money—subject to a successful exit. Only about 30% of companies in top-tier VC firms bring that kind of a return on average.

It is all about growth, stupid! So you don't have to be a Twitter, Facebook, Google or Instagram to bring good returns to your VC. You do, however, need to grow rapidly in customers and eventually revenue and profit as well. Your ability to instill confidence in your investor that with the money he/she gives your startup you can drive real growth, really fast is the best way to get your valuation up.

Many different valuation methods exist, and several could potentially be used in deciding on a startup's valuation. While all of them differ, and some or none of them may be relevant to your situation, it is better to at least be aware of them. You can Google them and study up as necessary.

- Comparables Method

- Venture Capital Method

- Step Up Method

- Earnings Multiplier Model

- Berkus Method

- Scorecard Valuation Method

- Risk Factor Summation Method

- Cost-to-Duplicate Method

- Discounted Cash Flow Method

- Valuation By Stage Method

- The Book Value Method

- First Chicago Method

Again while these methods do exist, I am not saying they are well used. Excluding the Comparables Method, they aren't. And if they are used, they are usually used as a weapon against a founder to bring valuation down. That said I always use the Comparables method, even if only for my own personal benchmark.

Comparables Method

This method is to look at the valuations of other similar startups, factoring in other ratios and multipliers for things that may not be similar between the two businesses.

For example, if Startup X is acquired for $8,000,000, and its website had 300,000 active users, you can estimate a valuation between the price of the startup and the number of users, which is $27/user. If Startup Z's business model is essentially the same as Startup X's and has 150,000 users, a justification could be made to allow it to use the same multiple of $27/user to reach a valuation of $4,000,000 (amounts have been rounded).

Personally, I use the Comparables Method to set upper and lower "anchors" on the price a startup can be valued at. If the list of several comparable startups has valuations ranging from $2 million to $28 million it becomes a relatively easy prospect to come up with (and justify) a valuation that is inside that range. It also signals to the investor that you won't take less than $2 million and won't be asking for more than $28 million (unless you can justify that with specific factors unique to your startup).

The idea is that there are companies out there similar enough to yours. Since at this stage you already have revenue, to get your valuation all we need to do is find out how many times valuation is bigger than revenue – or in other words, what the multiple is. That multiple we can get from these comparable companies. Once we get the multiple, we multiply your revenue by it, which produces your valuation.

To create your list of comparables you need to do some research. Several websites offer detailed information about startups and their funding successes. The first four are English language websites which most US and non-US startups are listed. But since the Chinese startup market is unique as it is now slightly larger than the US (both number of companies and funding amounts), you need to use ITJuzi or other Chinese resources to find those. Personally, I most often use CrunchBase and ITJuzi:

- CrunchBase

- ITJuzi (Language: Chinese)

- AngelList

- Gust

What to say when investors tell you "your valuation is too high."

First things first. Almost all investors will tell you this. It is just part of the haggling process, and they want to see how you respond. The key to deflecting this and getting to a decision (invest or not invest) is to find out the exact reason behind it. Common reasons for an investor saying your valuation is "too high" are:

Your valuation exceeds their investment fund criteria. If they say "your valuation is above the limit of our fund criteria. We only invest in startups with a valuation of 1 million or less." Most angel investors and early-stage VC firms only consider pitches from startups that are early-stage with valuations below certain limits. This is because a high valuation is usually almost always linked to a high raise amount. You need to ask the angels if they have such criteria before you begin negotiations.

The investor wants more Equity. If they say, "we like your startup and team, and we'd like to invest, but we need to get a bit more equity to offset the risk of the investment." This is usually a good sign. It means they want to engage and negotiate for a part of your company. It means "let's talk more."

The investor wants more Control. If they say, "this is a negotiation, and there needs to be some give and take." In response, if you can be flexible on other deal terms such as voting rights and board seats, investors might be willing to accept a higher valuation.

With startups once again please realize valuation is a negotiation—an art, not a science. Don't let anyone tell you otherwise.

Calculating Valuation.

The math itself is simple.

1. You assign a value to the startup. This is called the pre-money valuation (refer to the content in this chapter regarding the factors that you should consider)

2. Add the investment amount to the pre-money valuation to get to your post-money valuation

3. The equity percentage owned by each investor is their investment amount divided by the post-money valuation

Common Valuation Mistakes

Too Low, Too Early. Basically giving away too much of the company too soon for too little money. This will put off future investors and potentially seriously limit the viability of the startup.

Too High, Too Early. Obtaining a larger than normal valuation early from an enthusiastic investor when the product/service has no customers increase the likelihood of a future "down round" or flat-out rejection from more experienced investors once the product/service launches and the ramp up does not pan out as well as originally expected. Just in case you were wondering, a "Down Round" is a funding round where the founders are forced to accept investment at a lower valuation than what was set in the previous round. While not a death knell for a startup per se, it is not perceived as a good thing either and usually represents some loss of confidence in the startup's ability to create enough long-term value. Down rounds are often related to execution-related hiccups by the founders but can also be triggered by changes in the competitive landscape, other recent valuations of comparable companies, and also macroeconomic factors. For example, the number of down rounds increased after the financial crisis of 2008. Some very famous and successful companies such as VMWare and OpenTable experienced down rounds and ended up having successful IPOs afterward.

No Customer Validation. Unless you have an impeccable track record as a founder, it makes no sense at all to push for an outsized initial valuation before you have a product shipping or some other form of customer validation. Don't allow your large valuation become an albatross around your neck. See Chapter 5 for more information on how to get this validation in your MVP stage.

Not Knowing What You Don't Know. If, as a founding team, you have not "done this before" and will be mostly learning everything as you go (e.g. technology, people management, product management, sales and marketing skills, recruitment, IP management, etc.) your valuation should naturally be lower to reflect a higher than normal execution risk. If you get a high valuation but the team can't deliver the product and results, you will come to regret that high valuation and the expectations that come with it.

Being Overly Fixated On Valuation Amount. In many cases, if you have a solid investor that wants to invest quickly, it is often better to give up a few percentage points of equity than endlessly haggle over the valuation amount. That way you close the investment quicker, get the capital you need and can quickly get back to the task of growing your startup.

Raise Amount vs. Equity Disconnect. I often see a lot of first-time entrepreneurs show up a pitch contests saying things like, "We are seeking $500,000 for 5% of our company"without realizing this implies a valuation of $10,000,000. This kind of novice mistake is not only embarrassing, but it is also hard to recover from as it screams, "I don't know what I am doing!"

Answering questions about valuation.

Valuation is a negotiation, and you will be asked questions you need to be prepared to answer. Once the investor is having this discussion with you, they should be already interested in investing. If they aren't you can find out quickly by asking them as many questions as they ask you. Following are some typical scenarios.

Scenario 1: Investor has a cap on early-stage investment amounts. The main thing here is to understand better what range of investment is possible for the investor and to gauge his/her interest level further and fit as an investor for your startup.

INVESTOR: Your valuation is too high!

YOU: Do you have a limit on your investment amounts? What is the maximum you can invest in an early stage company?

INVESTOR: Yes we cap our investments at early stage startups at $2 million

YOU: Can you tell me what your best and worst performing investments were at the $2 million investment amount? I would like to understand your investment criteria and track record better.

Scenario 2: Investor wants more equity to offset the "risk." This type of question shows the investor is already interested in investing. You need to explore where the perceived risk and offset it by taking him/her through it.

INVESTOR: At this valuation, we need more equity to make the deal work for us.

YOU: What is the biggest risk you perceive? This is not a lot of money, and we run a very lean company.

INVESTOR: We think it will take longer to ramp up sales than you are forecasting.

YOU: I can take you through exactly what the money will be used for and how it will impact growth and sales execution.

Scenario 3: Investor wants more control to offset the "risk." This type of question shows the investor is concerned about the founding team's ability to execute or to control the exit strategy to some extent. This investor needs to be further vetted as to whether there is a good fit and the investor can bring his/her connections and experience to bear for the startup.

INVESTOR: At this valuation, we need (insert one or all: board seat, preferred share voting rights, etc.) to make the deal work for us.

YOU: Why is this important to you? What specific relationships and opportunities can you bring us to justify this request?

INVESTOR: I know people in the industry who can help you ramp up your sales (or build your product, etc.)

YOU: Can you introduce me to those people? I would like to get to know them and get a feel for what they are capable of.

Scenario 4: Investor claims your valuation is not in line with your current (low) revenues. This is likely pure haggling on price.

INVESTOR: Your valuation seems really high for a company earning under $10,000 a month in revenue right now.

YOU: This revenue stream is based on our MVP offering. Our current revenue streams prove there are customers who value the product enough to pay for it. The investment dollars will be used primarily to fund customer growth. You of all people should know that valuing our company on Discounted Cash Flow (DCF) terms at this early stage really does not make sense.

INVESTOR: I am not using DCF, I do think your business will grow fast enough.

YOU: We have a plan to get to 10 times these numbers leveraging the money you invest to get us by doing x,y,z... I am sure your investment would be more than justified if we were doing $100,000 a month, right? If we had 10x monthly revenues, we could easily justify a 2x higher valuation that we are asking for now. Are you saying you would be in at a higher valuation in that scenario?

These are a few of the common scenarios you will likely come across when negotiating your valuation. You will run into quite a few more as you go through the fundraising process. One thing you can do to increase your success rate in valuation negotiations (and any kind of negotiation, actually) is to spend some time studying the cognitive biases that we as human beings all share.

20 COGNITIVE BIASES THAT SCREW UP YOUR DECISIONS

1. Anchoring bias.

People are **over-reliant** on the first piece of information they hear. In a salary negotiation, whoever makes the first offer establishes a range of reasonable possibilities in each person's mind.

2. Availability heuristic.

People **overestimate the importance** of information that is available to them. A person might argue that smoking is not unhealthy because they know someone who lived to 100 and smoked three packs a day.

3. Bandwagon effect.

The probability of one person adopting a belief increases based on the number of people who hold that belief. This is a powerful form of **groupthink** and is reason why meetings are often unproductive.

4. Blind-spot bias.

Failing to recognize your own cognitive biases is a bias in itself. People notice cognitive and motivational biases much more in others than in themselves.

5. Choice-supportive bias.

When you choose something, you tend to feel positive about it, even if that **choice has flaws.** Like how you think your dog is awesome – even if it bites people every once in a while.

6. Clustering illusion.

This is the tendency to **see patterns in random events** It is key to various gambling fallacies, like the idea that red is more or less likely to turn up on a roulette table after a string of reds.

7. Confirmation bias.

We tend to listen only to information that confirms our **preconceptions** – one of the many reasons it's so hard to have an intelligent conversation about climate change.

8. Conservatism bias.

Where people favor prior evidence over new evidence or information that has emerged. People were **slow to accept** that the Earth was round because they maintained their earlier understanding that the planet was flat.

9. Information bias.

The tendency to **seek information** when it does not **affect action.** More information is not always better. With less information, people can often make more accurate predictions.

10. Ostrich effect.

The decision to **ignore dangerous or negative information** by "burying" one's head in the sand, like an ostrich. Research suggests that investors check the value of their holdings significantly less often during bad markets.

11. Outcome bias.

Judging a decision based on the **outcome** – rather than how exactly the decision was made in the moment. Just because you won a lot in Vegas doesn't mean gambling your money was a smart decision.

12. Overconfidence.

Some of us are **too confident about our abilities,** and this causes us to take greater risks in our daily lives. Experts are more prone to this bias than laypeople, since they are more convinced that they are right.

13. Placebo effect.

When **simply believing** that something will have a certain effect on you causes it to have that effect. In medicine, people given fake pills often experience the same physiological effects as people given the real thing.

14. Pro-innovation bias.

When a proponent of an innovation tends to **overvalue its usefulness** and undervalue its limitations. Sound familiar, Silicon Valley?

15. Recency.

The tendency to weigh the **latest information** more heavily than older data. Investors often think the market will always look the way it looks today and make unwise decisions.

16. Salience.

Our tendency to focus on the **most easily recognizable** features of a person or concept. When you think about dying, you might worry about being mauled by a lion, as opposed to what is statistically more likely, like dying in a car accident.

17. Selective perception.

Allowing our expectations to **influence how we perceive** the world. An experiment involving a football game between students from two universities showed that one team saw the opposing team commit more infractions.

18. Stereotyping.

Expecting a group or person to have certain qualities without having real information about the person. It allows us to quickly identify strangers as friends or enemies, but people tend to **overuse and abuse** it.

19. Survivorship bias.

An error that comes from focusing only on surviving examples, causing us to **misjudge a situation.** For instance, we might think that being an entrepreneur is easy because we haven't heard of all those who failed.

20. Zero-risk bias.

Sociologists have found that **we love certainty** – even if it's counterproductive. Eliminating risk entirely means there is no chance of harm being caused.

SOURCES: Brain Biases; Ethics Unwrapped; Explorable; Harvard Magazine; HowStuffWorks; LearnVest; Outcome bias in decision evaluation, Journal of Personality and Social Psychology; Psychology Today; The Bias Blind Spot: Perceptions of Bias in Self Versus Others, Personality and Social Psychology Bulletin; The Cognitive Effects of Mass Communication, Theory and Research in Mass Communications; The less-is-more effect: Predictions and tests, Judgment and Decision Making; The New York Times; The Wall Street Journal; Wikipedia; You Are Not So Smart; ZhurnalyWiki

Particularly useful for valuation negotiations is an in-depth understanding of the following biases: Anchoring, Zero-risk bias, Salience, Outcome, Information. In particular, when setting your valuation and going into the meeting, you need a plan to leverage the anchoring bias.

The <u>anchoring bias</u> refers to a human tendency to rely too heavily on the very first piece of information you learn. For example, you are told the average price for a car is a certain value; you will think any amount below that is a good deal, perhaps not searching for better deals. Conversely, this bias can be used to set the expectations of others by putting the first information on the table for consideration. With the valuation discussion, if you start with a valuation that is higher than what you will eventually accept that will provide become the anchor, and the investor will feel like they are getting a good deal if they talk you down a bit. That said, an experienced investor may well counter with an "extreme anchor"—an unbelievably low valuation—to throw you off and to dislodge the anchor you tried to set. The only way to get good at negotiation is to become familiar with the techniques by both reading about them and by actually practicing them in real life. There exists no pixie dust that will make you a great negotiator. It takes study and practice.

pixie dust

Definitions

from Wiktionary, Creative Commons Attribution/Share-Alike License

n. dust purported to be passively produced by pixies. It is represented as being magical in quality and can grant certain abilities to those who can obtain and harness its power.

At most of my startup MVP workshops, I typically end with the following slide that contains four books I feel every entrepreneur should read. With regards to negotiation, Chris Voss' book, "Never Split The Difference: negotiating as if your life depended on it" published by Harper Collins is far and away my favorite. And that is saying a lot as I have been selling since I was a child and have read most all the good books on this topic.

Takeaways:
"Get" Culture, Iterate Fast and...

Add my personal WeChat
Subscription account

Get the my articles and
complete reading list!

Read More Books!
(know what you don't know)

Not every investor you meet will want to invest, but you CAN endeavor to learn something from every investor you meet if you approach the meeting with the right attitude. You should leverage each meeting as a real-world chance to enhance your negotiation skills.

Tao Te Ching 道德经 Verse 33

Knowing others is intelligence; knowing yourself is true wisdom.

Mastering others is strength; mastering yourself is true power.

If you realize that you have enough, you are truly rich.

If you stay in the center and embrace death with your whole heart, you will endure forever.

10

INVESTOR MEETINGS

FACE TO FACE INVESTOR MEETINGS: BE THE BUDDHA

Every conversation with a potential investor is a chance to learn something. You had better look forward to these discussions as you will likely be having many of them. Most founders of famous companies (Google, Amazon, etc.) had to meet with more than 100 investors before getting that crucial first investment. In the meeting, you must come across as relaxed. Make it a real conversation. Try to find out what the investor wants and see if it matches well with your vision. Be the Buddha!

But before you go in make sure you know what you are capable of. The only way to find that out is by doing it. Even if you have not launched yet, build your MVP and work through the sales process and the user flow. Your confidence will come from the hard work you have done on the product offering. If you are already shipping and earning revenue, you need to work what you have to know what you need to get to the next level. There are three quotes I always come back to before I pitch an idea. They serve to level set me and put me in the right frame of mind for the discussion.

The key to success is to be so good they can't ignore you. - Steve Martin

This quote from Steve Martin needs to be your core mantra. If you are working your ass off, making the product/service better every day, interacting with customers and tweaking and trying new things you will be "so good" that the world will take notice of you. Testing yourself every day as Steve Martin did on stage with his new jokes, routines, and material to find out what works and what doesn't will give you the edge in the marketplace. It will also force you to hone your product and skills in real time.

You are almost always better off making your business better than making your pitch better - Marc Andresson

---

I see too many people fussing endlessly over their pitch and the style versus the substance of the pitch. If you know your business cold and can articulate your value proposition and respond in the moment to any question, you will undoubtedly do better than someone who is just another pretty pitch deck. Making your business better every day should be your number one focus, not pleasing investors. Meeting VCs is part luck and part numbers game. Look at each pitch as a "practice session," and you will not feel the need to sacrifice time that you should be spending on growing your business in endlessly prepping for investor meetings. Personally, I see Sequoia Capital as the ultimate savvy VC. However, I have never received funding from them. Therefore I see every VC meeting I have as a "practice session" for Sequoia. That way I have no pressure in any of the VC meetings I have and eventually when I do back a startup that receives money from Sequoia, I can honestly say I have spent the better part of my life practicing for it. This technique can work for you. Focusing on the practice versus the VC in front of your face to be successful is the essence of the what I think of as the "Tao of Startups," and it is why this book is so titled. Just like David Beckham when he makes a free kick or Micheal Jordan when someone passes him the ball. All their practice up to that moment allows them to execute well without having to necessarily think about it in the moment. Call it muscle memory, yoga or the Tao, but it is the practice you have put in that gets you to victory, not the actual act itself.

"RAISING VENTURE CAPITAL IS THE EASIEST THING A STARTUP FOUNDER IS EVER GOING TO DO. AS COMPARED TO RECRUITING ENGINEERS—IN PARTICULAR, RECRUITING ENGINEER NUMBER 20 IS FAR HARDER THAN RAISING VENTURE CAPITAL. SELLING TO ENTERPRISE CUSTOMERS IS HARDER. GETTING VIRAL GROWTH GOING ON A CONSUMER BUSINESS IS HARDER. GETTING ADVERTISING REVENUE IS HARDER. ALMOST EVERYTHING YOU'LL EVER DO IS HARDER THAN RAISING VENTURE CAPITAL. IF YOU GET IN A SITUATION WHERE RAISING MONEY IS HARD, IT'S PROBABLY NOT HARD COMPARED TO ALL THE OTHER STUFF THAT IS ABOUT TO FOLLOW. BEARING THIS IN MIND IS CRUCIAL. IT IS OFTEN SAID RAISING MONEY IS NOT ACTUALLY A SUCCESS, NOT ACTUALLY A MILESTONE FOR A COMPANY. I THINK THAT IS TRUE AND I THINK THAT IS THE UNDERLYING REASON. IT JUST PUTS YOU IN A POSITION TO DO ALL THE OTHER, HARDER THINGS." MARC ANDREESSEN. - LECTURE 9 - HOW TO RAISE MONEY - STANDFORD COURSE CS183 B

At the end of the day, VCs have their own interest at heart. The more you can do to show them you have a real business with real potential, the easier it will be to convince them to invest. Investor money shouldn't make or break your plans; it should only be a way for you to accelerate growth. Don't pin all your hopes on raising VC funds. Focus on building a quality business that scales and delights customers so that they come back and tell their friends about your company.

Evaluating Startup Potential

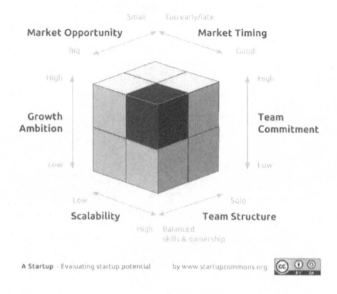

From the investor's point of view, it is really about team, idea, and execution. As an angel investor, mentor and entrepreneur, I have worked with hundreds of startups over the years. I try to evaluate opportunities using the matrix below.

Team	Idea	Execution	Angel Investor Reaction
Great	Great	Great	Sign me up! You are funded!
Great	Great	Terrible	You guys need help! Lets hire the right person and make this work!
Great	Terrible	Great	This startup isn't gonna work. Find another opportunity so you can crush it. Any ideas?
Great	Terrible	Terrible	I like you guys, why don't you come work for me?
Terrible	Great	Great	You guys have goon as far as you can take it. How about 100K for 51%? Take it or leave it.
Terrible	Great	Terrible	How about finders fee of 5% for this idea and your work so far and I will run with it?
Terrible	Terrible	Great	I have some PowerPoint slides that need cleaning up, how about $100 to fix them?
Terrible	Terrible	Terrible	I have to run to my next meeting, nice meeting you. Goodbye!

As you can see from the matrix, as long as the founding team is good there is a good chance I will be interested in them one way or the other. The quality of the idea (and the timing of the idea), as well as the team's execution ability, also factor in. But not as much as the quality of the team. I am not sure why this is but most of the people who attend my seminars or seek me out for help, mentorship or investment are solo founders. If you are a solo founder, I am happy to mentor you, but my first piece of advice will be to find a great co-founder! Finding the right co-founder(s) is so essential, yet seems to be so problematic for so many entrepreneurs that I regularly give seminars on this one topic alone.

Team

Building on the pitching points discussed in Chapter 3, the VC will be looking first and foremost at your team. They will watch your interaction, ask about your backgrounds, who will be doing what, etc.

Idea

This incorporates a lot including the scalability, market sizing as well as the actual core idea itself. This is where your research into what type of companies the VC has invested in previously and which types of solutions (hardware, software, consumer, enterprise, etc.) the VC has funded already.

Valuation

Whether you like it or not, if a VC is even mildly interested they will ask about your valuation. (see Chapter 9).
Research the pros/cons of "high" or "low" valuation. What you can get valuation-wise depends on your target investor and your track record. Angels rarely look at anything above $10 million.

Why Now?

From those that know, the most often asked question from Sequoia (again, my benchmark VC) is "Why Now?"

Why now?

Why this idea? Why me? Why now?

Why this idea? Think of a farmer's market. You take your product to the farmer's market, and either people buy or they don't. You either go home with a fistful of cash or you have to load all the stuff you brought to sell back up in your car and go home. The best part is that for minimal cost, you get to let 50-100 people test your product in one day. If the product doesn't sell, you will get immediate feedback, and the next time you come back to the farmer's market, you will have made the necessary tweaks.

So tell your VCs about the problem you are solving, the niche you serve. Give them anecdotes of how you conducted your farmer's market testing and how you tweaked the product based on that feedback. Doing this will make them feel more confident that you have a market and are on the right path.

Sequoia's partners ask the most critical questions in the age of the mass-produced startup: What has changed that makes this the perfect time for your startup to exist? Every great startup has a "Why now?" when you think about it.

Twitter's "Why now?" -- while everyone had read blogs created by tools such as WordPress and Blogger, more and more people felt they had something to say or communicate but not the technical skills or patience to write and manage a blog. Twitter allowed everyone to get involved in self-publishing.

YouTube's "why now?" -- massive reduction in bandwidth costs, the rapid proliferation of inexpensive video cameras and phones to record digital video files, and a new wave of smartphones with built-in cameras and an Internet connection.

Dropbox's "Why now?" -- the proliferation of data drove down the cost of storage meets the mass adoption of broadband in the office and home. Cloud technology made it on-demand and easy, and the freemium model combined with an innovative "invite a friend to use and get free storage capacity marketing campaign" made it wildly successful with the masses.

Uber's "Why now?" -- smartphone ubiquity, GPS accuracy, and increased usage of mobile apps combined with long-standing public dissatisfaction with standard taxi service.

Facebook's "Why now?" The massive ballooning of smartphone photography and the innocuous "Like" button combined with a ten-times faster, scalable and better-executed iteration of Friendster and MySpace.

I'm not sure every startup needs to have a killer "Why now?" but it seems like most do. Other key things are:

What is your unfair advantage? What is your "special sauce"? Are you an outlier? If you are pitching as if you are the next unicorn, then you need to explain why you are so entirely different.

Is your elevator pitch bulletproof? You need to be able to pitch your product. You need to be extremely good at it.

Is your company bootstrappable? How long can it survive without venture capital? What is your runway given your burn rate?

The Flow

When working with a large VC, there is usually a process that I call "the flow." The purpose of all VC meetings is to get another meeting (assuming you want one). It's not to push a decision. Therefore, understanding the general flow of the meeting process is critical for founders.

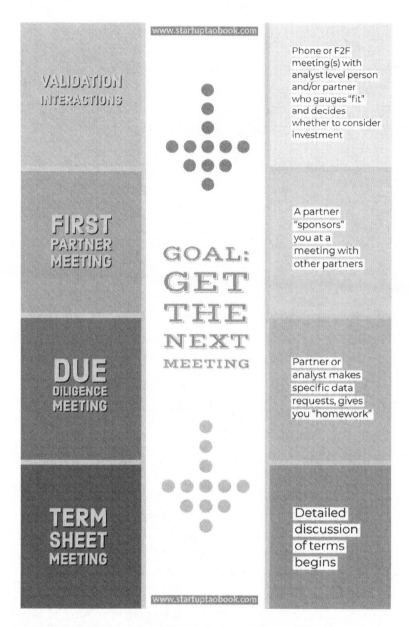

VALIDATION INTERACTIONS

Phone or F2F meeting(s) with analyst level person and/or partner who gauges "fit" and decides whether to consider investment

FIRST PARTNER MEETING

A partner "sponsors" you at a meeting with other partners

GOAL: GET THE NEXT MEETING

DUE DILIGENCE MEETING

Partner or analyst makes specific data requests, gives you "homework"

TERM SHEET MEETING

Detailed discussion of terms begins

First things first. Some VCs want you to hand over your pitch and your all kinds of facts and figures that don't need to be discussed until you get to the due diligence phase. I have a track record, so I typically do not give VCs anything before a meeting. The reason is simple; these are the things they mainly use to disqualify you before they spend time meeting you. If you have no track record and no personal connections (that will allow you to get an introduction via email, for example), then you will likely have to send something before they agree to meet you. That is what your pitch is for. Hopefully, you have taken my advice in Chapter 6, and you have a well-crafted pitch. Given that the average VC spends less than 4 minutes (3:44 on average to be exact) the real magic needs to happen in the room, and you can expect your VC to know next to nothing about what you do or what you want to pitch.

If your first meeting is with an analyst and not a partner, then the dynamics can be entirely different. The analyst is only concerned with looking good in the eyes of the partner he/she represents and not really interested in your company per se. As the analyst about the management structure and the decision process and don't be afraid to ask for their help to take the meeting to the next level. Ask them for feedback on your pitch is one way. Don't be afraid to ask point blank questions to get the analyst to commit to taking you to the next level. "You seem interested, can you and I meet with XXX partner later this week to get his/her feedback." Or you don't seem very interested, shall I assume your firm is not interested? I have a close friend who knows XXX partner. I wonder what he/she (partner name) will think about our product offering? You have nothing to lose, and you should make sure you learn as much as you can in the meeting. Analysts are not paid well and are not entrepreneurs. Except for maybe having attended a more prestigious school than you have, they certainly are not entrepreneurs like you.

Again, do not be afraid to ask questions and find out what you need to know.

The VC partner may, however, know quite a lot about the marketplace you are targeting. They may have invested in one of your "competitors." They may have any number of pre-conceived notions about lots of things. Therefore you need to prepare. Understand what stage of companies they typically invest in, what sectors they invest in. How long it has been since their last big exit and how long it has been since they raised a fund. You need to prepare some questions to ask them about what type of firm they are and the deals they tend to go for. You don't need to memorize things, just come up with 2-3 questions you would like to ask them based on your research. Just remember the questions you want to ask and make sure you get them answered. Mostly it is your job in the room to show them why you are "different," an outlier, the next big thing. Whether you do that using a powerpoint, whiteboard, napkin, a product demo or just by talking is up to you, and your style and the venue set up. You should be prepared to do all of the above as required.

First VC Meeting. Most likely with usually a junior analyst or just one VC partner, the purpose of this meeting is to validate the investment opportunity for the VC firm. Honestly, most times this is your first and last meeting with the VC as they use it to decide whether or not to pursue your startup as an investment opportunity seriously. Whether it was the personal referral or the pitch deck you sent that caught their eye, all VC conversations start at this point. So regardless of how you want the meeting to go, the purpose is not to ask for a commitment immediately. Instead, the goal is to get a follow-up meeting with a partner who can decide on the investment or can sponsor it at the VC's investment committee meeting. Therefore it is paramount that you ask the people you meet what the normal decision process is at their VC firm. In my experience, there are more than a few VC firms that via the questions they ask or the way they ask them that may cause you not to pursue a follow-up meeting with that VC. Follow your gut here. Remember you are giving them the opportunity to invest in your startup. They need to do their part of selling you as well.

   Diligence Meetings. Once one or two partners have decided the investment is worth pursuing further, the process moves on to the "diligence" phase – the partner may give the founder specific data requests, validation meetings, and phone calls led by the original VC partner to further confirm that the opportunity is worth pursuing further. This can be a bit disorienting to the founder as it is hard to know if the process is progressing or not. The most visible signal to watch is whether the VC is getting increasingly excited or not. If the diligence period ends up not discouraging the VC from investing, the next phase is a partner meeting where another partner or two comes in to play devil's advocate.

   Partner Meeting. This is where first "decision" is made. You could say that every previous meeting is equally as important as this one, as they're all interconnected, but this first partner meeting is the most important single interaction. This is especially the case in larger partnerships where some people are hearing your story first-hand for the first time. Usually, by this point, the lead partner has morphed into a full-on advocate for the investment and may even offer up tips and guidance on navigating this meeting effectively. Nonetheless, the outcome can be more volatile as one partner sitting on the fence or one adamantly opposed can swing the decision against the investment. This is the first meeting where an entrepreneur conveys the direct "ask" and pushes for an immediate, definitive decision on investment. If there indeed is mutual interest and, after any normal back and forth around the specific ask concludes, the next step is to hold a meeting to finalize the term sheet quickly.

Term Sheet Meeting. Once a VC firm has made a decision internally to invest, they don't want to lose out on the opportunity. Quickly the tables turn, and the VC requests a follow-up in-person meeting to present a term sheet, talk through terms, sell their firm, and also sometimes conduct some remaining high-level due diligence.

If you approach fundraising and investor meetings as a necessary evil and a chore, it will be. I guarantee you. However, if you approach it as a way to validate your business model and test your assumption with (mostly) intelligent and market-savvy people, then the time you spend will be incredibly valuable.

Make sure you ask as many questions as you get asked. You need to evaluate the investor as much as he/she needs to assess you and your startup. Make notes of learnings and actions from each meeting. Document the key points discussed and follow up with an email or other communication restating these and the next steps within the day you meet. Remember the investor meets lots of startups, it is up to you to drive the momentum as to the extent you can, set the agenda.

Tao Te Ching 道德经 Verse 64

What is rooted is easy to nourish.

What is recent is easy to correct.

What is brittle is easy to break.

What is small is easy to scatter.

Prevent trouble before it arises.

Put things in order before they exist.

The giant pine tree grows from a tiny sprout.

The journey of a thousand miles starts from beneath your feet.

Rushing into action, you fail.

Trying to grasp things, you lose them.

Forcing a project to completion, you ruin what was almost ripe.

Therefore the Master takes action by letting things take their course.

He remains as calm at the end as at the beginning.

He has nothing, thus has nothing to lose.

What he desires is non-desire; what he learns is to unlearn.

He simply reminds people of who they have always been.

He cares about nothing but the Tao.

Thus he can care for all things.

11

THE DUE DILIGENCE

DUE DILIGENCE: BE FUNDABLE!

When you do find an investor that is right for you and you want to accept their money, you need certain things prepared: bank accounts, legal entity, etc. These things all need to be done and ready before you talk to investors. However, I find many first-time entrepreneurs spend too much time on them because doing them feels like checking off items on a checklist. Please make sure you prioritize these things correctly and get them done at the right time.

Some startups hire a law firm to handle the incorporation process for them. A good law firm or attorney will walk you through many of the decisions we cover in this chapter (but not all). They will also generate the relevant documents (Certificate of Incorporation, Bylaws, Initial Board Consent, stock purchase agreements, etc.), and for U.S. companies file your Certificate of Incorporation with Delaware (or other jurisdiction). Some firms will help with other details such as getting a Federal Employer Identification Number (EIN) and arranging a registered agent (a third-party registered within the state who receives all physical correspondence from the state on your company's behalf).

However, it is more likely that you will have to do these things on your own. In the U.S. and many other countries, these can be done quickly and cheaply online.

Because much of the process can be done online, in the U.S. and in many countries around the world law firms are not willing to do these "company formation things" as they require lots of activities, running around and are certainly not as profitable as their core business. Furthermore, your cousin's uncle's law firm may also not have any specific experience in doing these things for startups and give you the wrong advice or make a mistake that will cost the company later. Also, many founders do not have or cannot justify spending several thousand dollars on these things in the early stages of a startup. For these and other reasons, many startup founders take at "Do It Yourself" or "DIY" approach. There is much valuable learning in the process, and I encourage first-time founders to do all or as much of it yourself. If you don't do it yourself, you must realize that time or money you save/spend in the beginning will almost always be offset by you having to step in and "find out" what was done by whomever you outsourced it to. For the DIY'ers there are lots of free resources available at CooleyGo, and this is one site I use frequently. If you must outsource then in the U.S., you can use UpCounsel to hire a free-lance attorney to help you with company formation, where you can expect to pay $1,000 to $2,000. Higher-end law firms often charge more than $5,000 for company formation. If you are a purely online business, it also pays to consider Stripe Atlas. For $500, Stripe will incorporate your company, arrange the registered agent, create your federal EIN, and even open a bank account for you. Outside the U.S. use a company that has a good reputation and experience and make sure you talk to at least one of their customers—get a reference!

Pre-Shareholder's Agreement

First things first! The Pre Shareholder Agreement (I call it the "Pre-SHA") is the first document I sign with my potential co-founders when we decide to seriously think about developing the idea into an MVP. Below is the document I use with all my startups. You can download this template from the website for this book. Simple, yet effective, once you are through high-fiving each other and begin to start buying domain names for your next Unicorn idea, be sure to take a few minutes to get this Pre-SHA signed. You will be glad you did.

Pre-Shareholder Agreement

Parties:

1. Founder 1 Name / City, State, Country / email address / mobile phone number
2. Founder 2 Name / City, State, Country / email address / mobile phone number
3. Founder 3 Name / City, State, Country / email address / mobile phone number

Terms of agreement

1. Parties have agreed to work together on a concept named "Working Company Name".
2. Parties are hereby agreeing that all the IPR and learnings that have been generated prior to and during the Agreement period that relate to concept, belong to the yet to be formed company (hereafter "WCN") with similar name to that stated in item 1 above.
3. In case of any IPR where by law, the individual has rights to IPR that cannot be transferred (copyright text, audio, etc.), WCN will get unlimited license to use any such IPR for free.
4. Any created, registered, etc., IPR that cannot be copied or licensed to multiple party (i.e. domain name, etc.), regardless to whose name it's been registered, who paid for it etc. cannot be used by any party individually, unless separately agreed by all parties. Any accumulated costs known to parties need to be balanced out, equally between parties for this clause to remain effective.
5. The parties will negotiate in good faith on follow up agreements needed for further development of the concept.

Agreement period

Effective from _____ until _____

Signatures

_____   _____   _____

Company Registration

In some countries (like China for example) it matters where you legally register your company as the services and support you can get from the local government varies widely. In the US, while you can register in your home state, you shouldn't. In the U.S., most startups are incorporated in

Delaware, and that's where investors expect your company to be incorporated. The reason being that the state has a long tradition of hosting major U.S. corporations, and has developed a well-defined body of law that's business-friendly. Even more so, Delaware is what everyone (investors, lawyers, accelerators, etc.) is familiar with and expects. In the U.S. If you don't incorporate in Delaware, then you are asking for trouble and complications in the future. So if you are in the U.S. and you are creating a high-growth startup, you should always go with a Delaware C-Corporation.

Bank Account

As soon as you have formed the company, the company needs a bank account. My only advice here is that you choose a bank nearby as you will likely have to go there in person more often than you think to arrange things. If possible, choose a larger bank with overseas branches. Larger banks with overseas branches tend to be more familiar with international banking, wire transfers and other aspects of business banking.

Number of Shares to Authorize

When you register a company, you need to decide how many shares to authorize. It can be any number, but for most companies amount should be 10 million. Why do you ask? That is because in the U.S. that is what everyone else does. It is a common precedent, a rule of thumb if you will. Also, 10 million is an easily divisible number, and it is a big enough number that when you give an employee 10,000 stock options, to them, it psychologically feels like a lot (even though it's only 0.1% of the company). It's also convenient when dealing with the price per share—if your company has a $10 million valuation, each share is worth $1. So for the U.S. authorize 10 million shares because that's the norm for startups. In other countries make sure you follow whatever guidelines are out there.

Number of Shares to Issue

There is a difference between authorizing shares and issuing shares. "Authorizing shares" is merely deciding how big (numerically) the pie should be. "Issuing shares" refers to cutting the pie into slices and handing some of them out. Once you decide how many shares to authorize, the next step is to determine how many shares to issue to the founding team.

Many people tend to overthink this, but I suggest allocating half of the authorized shares to you and your cofounders. Doing things this way should give you enough shares available to make it through your Series A round without having to authorize additional shares.

Let's look at an example. Let's say we issued 4 million shares to the founding team and set aside 1 million shares into an option pool for future hires. We've now carved out 5 million shares. In order to get to a Series A funding round, and assuming you may have two prior rounds (for example, pre-seed and seed), and during those "prior rounds" give away 20%-30% of the company each round. Therefore if we start out with 5 million shares and are then diluted 25% over three consecutive funding rounds, you are still within your original 10 million authorized shares:

$5,000,000 \times 1.25 = 6,250,000$

$6,250,000 \times 1.25 = 7,812,500$

$$7{,}812{,}500 \times 1.25 = 9{,}765{,}625$$

Creating the Cap Table

In the early days of a startup, this is probably the most document you will create. A capitalization table (cap table) tells you "who owns what" in the startup. There are five kinds of people on a cap table: founders, employees, advisors, angels, and VCs. At its most basic level, a cap table is just a list of your company's securities (i.e., stock, options, warrants, etc.) and who owns those securities. The very first version will likely only contain the founders and the amount of stock each owns. Even if you hate "doing spreadsheets" and don't even have a budget document, you need a cap table because, as an entrepreneur, you will constantly be making decisions that impact your capitalization quite frequently. For example, if you are considering taking on a new investor, you need to be able to quickly run scenarios based on different pre-money valuations, different investment amounts, etc. Alternatively, if you are recruiting a CTO and need to offer stock or stock options, you need to be able to quickly determine how dilutive the new stock grant will be to other owners and what percentage of total company ownership that grant represents. An accurate and well-organized cap table will enable a founding team to make good decisions quickly. There are a few things about managing the cap table you should take to heart. First of all the cap table is not a "communal document" and should not be shared on Google Docs or a similar service. The founding team should empower only one person (usually the CEO) with the right to create, manage and update the document. It should be managed in Microsoft Excel (as this is the tool that is usable and readable by most people and devices) and each version should be date-labeled and distributed to all of the people on the cap table. Since this type of document is widely used, samples and templates can be found for free download on many websites, including at CooleyGo mentioned previously. Recently, some companies offer cap table creation and management services in the cloud (as well as a host of other services concerning your company's shares). Call me "old school," but this makes no sense to me. As a founder, you want this document in your possession and by the time your company is big enough to warrant third-party services managing shares, shareholders, all the transactions, agreements and so forth you will likely not be the person doing that for your startup anyway. CooleyGo is a good, no-nonsense and legally sound reference. There are too many services offering to help you create and "manage" your cap table. Avoid them. Search the Internet to find a good, simple template and do it yourself. Anything beyond you typing into an Excel template for a cap table is overkill.

Components of the Cap Table

Following are the terms you need to understand to create and manage your cap table.

Authorized Shares: The total number of all the shares of stock that the company can issue. The number is set in the company's articles of incorporation. For typical startup companies, this number is in the low seven-figure range (10,000,000 is recommended).

Outstanding Shares: These are the shares of stock that have been issued and are held by the stockholders (e.g., founders in the first version of the cap table).

Shares Reserved for Stock Option Plan: These shares are often referred to as the "option pool." They are not outstanding shares (as no stockholder holds them), but they are set aside, for later issuance by the company when stock options are exercised. Typically, the size of the pool at the formation stage ranges between 10% and 20% percent of the fully diluted shares (see explanation below). Also note that other forms of equity compensation, such as stock awards, may also be granted from this pool but in the early days of the startup this is irrelevant.

Remaining Unissued Shares: The authorized shares that are leftover; shares that are available for the company to issue and that are not otherwise reserved (unlike the shares reserved for the stock option plan). Having some remaining unissued shares can be useful in the future if the company wants to issue additional stock to a new co-founder or reserve more shares for the pool without filing an amendment to its charter. However, it's a good rule of thumb to not have more than half of the company's authorized shares unissued. Otherwise, the company could owe a significantly higher annual franchise tax (specifically in Delaware) and could present future ownership risks and issues.

Fully Diluted Shares: The number of shares that would be outstanding if all possible sources of stock were converted or exercised. Investors, prefer to see their ownership expressed in terms of fully diluted shares to conservatively determine the value of their shares, assuming that the entire pool will be used and any options, warrants and convertible notes will be exercised or converted. Note that the percentage of fully diluted shares will typically be lower than the percentages of the founders split.

For drafting a cap table for a new startup, that's all the founders should need to know. As the company grows and evolves to higher levels of complexity, so will its cap table, but the fundamentals of its anatomy explained here will remain the same.

Due Diligence

In the process of interacting with VC firms or more established Angels who show an interest in your startup, you will likely be asked to present some data for "due diligence" In most cases this isn't a formal legal or technical diligence; rather, it's VC speak for "I'm taking my investment consideration to the next level." Depending on what the VC asks for, this "due diligence" can be very costly in terms of founder time spent preparing. In most cases, this time could be better spent on the business so be careful regarding what you commit to providing. During this phase, a VC may ask for many things, such as sales and marketing plans, projections, customer pipeline or targets, product development plans, competitive (SWOT) analysis, and founding team bios. This is all relatively normal. Some VCs will accept what you have already created in the running of your business and in anticipation of the financing. Other VCs may ask you spend a significant amount of time providing information in a format that suits their needs. In any event, before you commit to doing the work, make sure a partner-level person is involved. Don't fall into the trap of doing the work that an associate at the VC firm is supposed to do.

Term Sheet

Once you have a cap table and begin talking to investors, you should already be thinking in a general sense regarding what terms you care about and which ones you can negotiate away. As far as investment is concerned, the term sheet is critical as it usually determines the final deal structure. Even though it is not binding, it is more than just a letter of intent. It is the basis for your startup's future relationship with your investor.

A term sheet is defined as a nonbinding agreement that covers the basic terms and conditions under which an investment will be made. The reasons for doing a simple term sheet before drafting detailed and expensive contracts are clear. A term sheet ensures that the parties involved in a business transaction agree on the key aspects of the deal, thereby avoiding future misunderstandings. Negotiating the term sheet first allows the principals in the negotiation to come to terms on the business details before the lawyers getting involved. In most cases, the real negotiation should be done at the term sheet phase. Beware of investors who try to negotiate hard and change terms via the longer, binding agreements that follow the term sheet. If you have never negotiated a term sheet before, I suggest you do your homework. For this, in particular, I highly recommend, "Venture Deals: Be Smarter Than Your Lawyer and Venture Capitalist" by Brad Feld and Jason Mendelson, Wiley Publishers. The book was published in 2011, so it is starting to show its age, but I really like the way the authors take the startup founder's point of view. You can find some more recent advice on the internet but Brad Feld in his work with TechStars (a very successful startup accelerator) has seen it all, and even though he is a VC in his own right, the book gives a solid entrepreneur's perspective to dealing with VCs. The book's website has a link to a number of useful online resources including downloadable contract templates, etc.

Accounting and Financial

Whether you can or want to do them, many financial-related functions must be done for your company. All my companies and successful founders I have been involved with have outsourced some or all of these tasks to bookkeeper, a bookkeeping company, a part-time or full-time employee, or a "drop-in" financial consultant. For your startup, this can be as simple as engaging a freelance bookkeeper (perhaps someone recommended by another startup friend) to come in once a month, take all the financial receipts from the shopping bag into which you have thrown them, and enter them into your system, plus reconciling the bank statements as they come in. As your startup grows, the visits naturally become weekly as there is more to do. Usually, after you've raised your first seed round, you should have enough work to keep a full-time bookkeeper busy on your payroll. If you do bring someone on to handle things, be sure to avoid giving that one person the power to disburse funds and balance the books. Failing to observe this leaves you wide open to fraud and embezzlement.

I always suggest you have a serious interview with any company or person you will have to "do your books." Take the time to meet them and ask them direct questions such as:

- What exactly do you do for your clients each month?

- Give me an example of a specific problem you have helped one of your clients solve that actually saved them money. Can I speak with that client for a reference?

- Outside of preparing company tax return to the best of your abilities, what else can you do for me that helps me grow my company?

- What other clients do you have that are in the same industry as I am?

- What do you do daily, weekly, monthly for these clients?

While you have this discussion, take note of your impressions. Could this person be a true partner in building your business? If yes, give them a try (pending reference checks). If not, break the meeting off politely and leave.

Among the tasks that this person will undertake are:

- Prepare monthly, quarterly, and annual financial reports.

- Work with co-founders to manage your financial projections.

- Prepare financial documents for potential investors.

- Create and manage budgets and offer the co-founding financial advice and guidance on meeting budget targets.

- Prepare your company's tax returns and dealing with the Internal Revenue Service (or your local tax authorities) if required.

- Prepare audited financial statements as requested or required by existing investors or for due diligence for prospective investors.

If your bookkeeper, financial consultant or accountant uses one of the many online accounting solutions, then you can ask for a login so that you can see your books online as well:

- www.netsuite.com

- quickbooks.intuit.com

- www.xero.com

- sage.com

- soncur.com

- accountedge.com

- waveapps.com

Payment Platforms

If you transact business online (highly recommended that you do!) then in the U.S. there are three main players in the field, each of which processes billions of dollars in transactions every year. However, because each is optimized for a slightly different purpose, you should compare their focus and pick the one that best suits your situation. The biggest of the three is Braintree, which is owned by PayPal.* This service can handle virtually any payment vehicle on the planet, from credit cards to PayPal to Venmo to Bitcoin. It is very powerful, has scaled pricing that drops as your volume increases, and is suitable for companies with in-house programming capabilities. The most startup-oriented of the three is Stripe, which provides flat-rate pricing, simple tools for integration into your website, and good customer service. The most straightforward and most mobile-friendly is Square, which is best if you plan to sell products in person and accept physical credit cards, or do not have a programmer on staff. While all three services offer point-of-sale credit card readers, Square's is a free, slick, tiny device that plugs into your mobile phone's headphone jack. It also has a small, battery-powered, Bluetooth-connected reader that can accept the new chip-and-PIN cards, as well as the contactless Apple Pay and Android Pay systems.

- www.braintreepayments.com

- stripe.com

- squareup.com

For startups which serve markets outside the U.S., you will know what platforms are best for your market. For example in China, AliPay and WeChat are even more advanced and more straightforward to implement than the platforms listed above.

Company Contracts

Lack of familiarity with legal contracts makes startup founders want to put all this "contract stuff" off until later. In the creation phase to focus on the vision for your startup and creating your MVP, once you know what you will be doing— hopefully, sooner rather than later—it's crucial that founders take the time to cover their legal bases. The following are the seven core legal documents that founders need to put in place to avoid costly legal battles in the future.

Articles of Incorporation. This was covered previously in this chapter under "Company Registration." In the process of registering your company, you will need to create this document.

Shareholders Agreement. At the time that equity is split, all co-founders should sign a shareholders agreement cum operating agreement. Fundamentally, the agreement should define the stock ownership ratios, the relationship of the founders, provide the expectation that all work product will belong to the entity, and outline a basic communication and conflict-resolution clause that helps prevent disputes and provides a process for dispute resolution.

Non-Disclosure Agreements. Having a non-disclosure agreement (NDA) for your company that is signed not only by employees but also potential partners is necessary. In practice, before any sensitive business conversations take place between you and an outside party you need to sign a mutual NDA. For any new partners or employees, you need to have an NDA agreement waiting for them to sign. NDAs allow you to safeguard your co-founder's and employees' ideas and your intellectual property. An NDA should specify the following:

- What specifically constitutes confidential information

- How confidential information should be handled

- Who owns that information (e.g., the company)

- The time period that the information will be disclosed

- The time period confidentiality will be maintained

Intellectual Property (IP) Assignment Agreement. This is especially vital for technology companies since much of the value of the company will be from the product and the technology behind it. Some other types of startups may be able to do without this agreement, but since anything created in the startup (including processes, methodologies, publications, ordering systems, etc.) can be construed as IP, in my opinion, all companies should have this type of contract in place.

To avoid costly claims filed by patent trolls and companies trying to copy your business model, the startup should have complete ownership of all IP assets in writing. When forming the company, it is wise to assign all relevant intellectual property to the company. There are two types of IP assignment agreements to consider:

Technology Assignment Agreements are for assigning to the startup company any intellectual property created before forming the company. Do this early as some technical people the startup contracts with may insist on retaining individual IP ownership rights, or they may attempt to sell their rights in exchange for equity or cash.

Invention Assignment Agreements are for assigning to the new company IP ownership of any relevant work product created by employees after the company's formation. A confidentiality and invention assignment agreement is typically signed by the founder(s) and employees. The company will own all rights to the IP portfolio created by the individuals working for the startup.

Bylaws. These are simple rules to establish the internal operational decision-making process of the company. For example, how to settle disputes, select leadership and determine the rights and powers of shareholders. Even more importantly, bylaws should institute voting thresholds for approvals to specific actions by the corporation like electing new board members or entering into debt.

Employee Contracts and Offer Letters

It really goes without saying, but startup CEOs and founders should draw up clear employment contracts and offer letters when hiring new employees. These documents are essential to ensure employees understand what's expected of them. The format is flexible, and you can find many templates on the internet, but the following should be clearly stated:

- Terms of employment (e.g., compensation, role, responsibilities, working hours and grounds for termination)

- Reporting structure (who does the employee report to and whom does he/she manage)

- IP ownership of work (in most cases this requires stating they will not have any IP rights to work product created while in the employ of the company)

- Expectations, KPIs, goals, requirements, etc.

- Shares granted and vesting schedule (if applicable)

- Company policies (e.g., vacation days, paid time off, dress code, code of conduct, etc.)

Shareholder Agreements

While equity holding should be decided and documented early in the life cycle of a startup in the cap table, when a startup is ready to take on private investments, the startup CEO should create a shareholder agreement that determines the rights of shareholders and defines when they can exercise those rights. Those rights can include shareholders' right to transfer shares, right of first refusal, redemption upon death or disability and shareholders' power to manage and run the startup. It is also imperative for founders to document the sale of any shares to avoid substantial financial penalties under state and federal laws.

"Cleaning Up" Founder's Social Media Presence

You may have been a hard-partying player in college or have a strange sense of humor and like playing practical jokes on friends and telling everyone about them on Facebook. Or maybe you have experimented with cross-dressing. Whatever your personal life and your social media persona have been to date, you need to take a serious look at cleaning up anything that exists on social media that could negatively impact your startup. This is more serious than you think. Because lots of pictures and things you say can be misinterpreted, especially if taken out of context could undermine your prospects for success. Because investors fundamentally invest in founders, not products, you can expect to be Googled extensively by any VC that may be considering investing in your startup. Google yourself and make sure you are OK with what you find. If not, proactively do something about it.

While time is a precious resource for any startup, I have outlined the key things (in the proper order) that founders need to do in order to put their legal and financial house in order. These things should not be put off until the first potential investor shows up because by that time it might very well be too late. All startup founder should prioritize putting these agreements into place to secure their company's future.

Tao Te Ching 道德经 Verse 81

True words aren't eloquent;

eloquent words aren't true.

Wise men don't need to prove their point;

men who need to prove their point aren't wise.

The Master has no possessions.

The more he does for others, the happier he is.

The more he gives to others, the wealthier he is.

The Tao nourishes by not forcing.

By not dominating, the Master leads.

CONCLUSION

Okay just because the last chapter in this book dealt with all the "boring and tedious" due diligence stuff, I don't want you putting it down thinking it is all too hard, or there are just too many things to remember. Net/net you do need to know all this stuff in the book, but since you have bought it, you can always come back to it and revisit the parts you need to brush up on.

As I mentioned in the forward, the genesis of this book was a presentation I have to give at a China Accelerator 8x8 Event on March 24, 2018, in Beijing in an event in front of a packed house of 200 current and future entrepreneurs. The time was limited to 8 minutes, and I gave myself the challenge to impart the most useful information these people would need in the allotted time. The result is that the content is well-organized (if I don't say so myself) both in the chronological order, a would-be entrepreneur needs to know the information, as well as content-wise. Each chapter focuses on a key thing every would-be entrepreneur needs to think about, do or create. The actual presentation was recorded. Feel free to have a look or visit www.startuptaobook.com which is the official website for this book and contains a lot of free supplemental information, videos, links, presentations, and the bibliography for this book.

Hopefully, this book has given you the confidence and the information you need to get out there and start your startup. Whether your answer is yes or no, I suggest you go back to Chapter 1 and review the section entitled: "Are you ready?" and review the 10 things you need to do to be successful in doing a startup."

Now, as it did when I first read it, this statement affects me deeply.

EVERY MOMENT IN BUSINESS HAPPENS ONLY ONCE. THE NEXT BILL GATES WILL NOT BUILD AN OPERATING SYSTEM. THE NEXT LARRY PAGE OR SERGEY BRIN WON'T MAKE A SEARCH ENGINE. AND THE NEXT MARK ZUCKERBERG WON'T CREATE A SOCIAL NETWORK. IF YOU ARE COPYING THESE GUYS, YOU AREN'T LEARNING FROM THEM. OF COURSE, IT'S EASIER TO COPY A MODEL THAN TO MAKE SOMETHING NEW. DOING WHAT WE ALREADY KNOW HOW TO DO TAKES THE WORLD FROM 1 TO N, ADDING MORE OF SOMETHING FAMILIAR. BUT EVERY TIME WE CREATE SOMETHING NEW, WE GO FROM 0 TO 1. THE ACT OF CREATION IS SINGULAR, AS IS THE MOMENT OF CREATION, AND THE RESULT IS SOMETHING FRESH AND STRANGE." - THIEL, PETER; MASTERS, BLAKE. ZERO TO ONE: NOTES ON STARTUPS, OR HOW TO BUILD THE FUTURE (P. 1). THE CROWN PUBLISHING GROUP.

This is exactly why I have found doing startups so immensely rewarding in my life. It is the "creation" part. Doing something that has never been done before. And that is why I do it because I like creating things that are fresh and strange. What are you waiting for? With this book, I have done my best to give you the keys to the kingdom. The rest is up to you. You will never know unless you try.

ABOUT THE AUTHOR

James LaLonde started his career as an early employee of Microsoft Japan and led the subsidiary's rise to the first billion-dollar revenue subsidiary of a software company in history. After his nearly 15 year corporate career which culminated in a role as CEO of a NASDAQ listed software company, James decided to become an entrepreneur and started RTM Asia.

Currently based in Beijing, James has co-founded 3 companies in China in the last 5 years. The first, Yodo1, is now the largest private publisher of mobile phone games in China.

The second, yoli, is the innovative new way to learn English or Mandarin all in WeChat; bringing the study anywhere, anytime Uber-style model to language learning.

The third, The Belt and Road Advisory (BRA) seeks to educate the world about China's Belt and Road Initiative. The Belt and Road Initiative (BRI) is history's largest infrastructure and trade route build out and is impacting the lives of billions of the world's inhabitants. Via BRA's analysis, blog, and podcast we deliver this knowledge to both Chinese and English speaking audiences. Furthermore, BRA offers professional advisory services on all matters concerning the Belt and Road Initiative.

A lifelong lover of people, culture, languages, reading and writing; James has published a best-selling business book in Japanese and writes regular articles in Chinese for his own WeChat account and other media.

James believes teaching others is the final step in the learning process. To that end, he is a frequent speaker and conductor of workshops all over China on entrepreneurial topics. In fact, this book, "The Tao of Startups" originated from just such a speaking engagement.

James is also a professor at the University of International Business and Economics in Beijing. He teaches an undergraduate course entitled "Entrepreneurship 201."

For more information on James see his LinkedIn profile or follow him on Twitter or the Tao of Startups Facebook page. For those of you in China, James' WeChat ID is: WJamesL

BIBLIOGRAPHY

The following is a partial list of books that I have read that are relevant in some way to this book's subject matter. They are listed no particular order. The online bibliography can be found on the <u>website for this book</u> is updated and contains embedded links to most of the books referenced:

- Too Big To Know: Rethinking Knowledge Now That the Facts Aren't The Facts, Experts are Everywhere and the Smartest Person in the Room Is the Room – David Weinberger

- Start with Why: How Great Leaders Inspire Everyone to Take Action – Simon Sinek

- The 80/20 Principle: The Secret to Achieving More with Less – Richard Koch

- The Lean Startup – Eric Ries

- The Startup Way – Eric Ries

- Zen in the Art of Archery – Herrigal Eugen

- The Art of the Startup Fundraising: Pitching Investors, Negotiating the Deal, and Everything Else Entrepreneurs Need to Know – Alejandro Cremades

- Principles: Life and Work – Ray Dalio

- Zero to One: Notes on Startups, or How to Build the Future – Peter Theil and Blake Masters

- Original version of "Finding Co-Founders" Presentation – James LaLonde

- Shoe Dog: A Memoir by the Creator of Nike – Phil Knight

- Thinking, Fast and Slow – Daniel Kahneman

- Never Split the Difference: Negotiating As If Your Life Depended On It – Chris Voss

- Debt – Updated and Expanded: The First 5,000 Years – David Graeber

- The Startup Checklist: 25 Steps to a Scalable, High-Growth Business – David S. Rose

- Angel: How to Invest in Technology Startups-Timeless Advice from and Angel Investor Who Turned $100,000 into $100,000,000 – Jason Calacanis

- Startup Evolution Curve From Idea to Profitable and Scalable Business: Startup Marketing Manual – Dr. Donatas Jonikas

- Peak: Secrets from the New Science of Expertise – Anders Ericsson

- The San Francisco Fallacy: The Ten Fallacies That Make Founders Fail – Jonathan Siegel

- Develop Your Idea!: Get off to a flying start with your startup. Guided exercises & resources for exploring and validating new businesses... – K.N. Kukoyi

- Scale: The Universal Laws of Growth, Innovation, Sustainability, and the Pace of Life in Organisms, Cities, Economies and Companies – Geoffrey West

- Scaling Lean: Mastering the Key Metrics for Startup Growth – Ash Maurya

- My Life and Work (The Autobiography of Henry Ford) – Henry Ford

- Measure What Matters – John Doerr

- The Complete Works of Epictetus – Epictetus

- The Ultimate Guide to Pricing Strategy – Alexander Shartsis

- The Startup J Curve: The Six Steps to Entrepreneurial Success – Howard Love

- The Airbnb Story: How Three Ordinary Guys Disrupted an Industry, Made Billions...and Created Plenty of Controversy – Leigh Gallagher

- Let it Go – Pat Flynn

- Tao of Charlie Munger: A Compilation of Quotes from Berkshire Hathaway's Vice Chairman on Life, Business and the Pursuit of Wealth... – David Clark

- Venture Deals: Be Smarter Than Your Lawyer and Venture Capitalist – Brad Feld and Jason Mendelson

- The Deming Management Method: The Best Selling Classic for Quality Management – Mary Walton

- The Innovators: How a Group of Hackers, Geniuses, and Geeks Created the Digital Revolution – Walter Isaacson

- The Zero Marginal Cost Society: The Internet of Things, the Collaborative Commons, and the Eclipse of Capitalism – Jeremy Rifkin

- Tools of Titans: The Tactics, Routines, and Habits of Billionaires, Icons and World Class Performers – Timothy Ferris

- The ONE Thing: The Surprisingly Simple Truth Behind Extraordinary Results – Gary Keller and Jay Papasan

- The Customer-Funded Business: Start, Finance, or Grow Your Company with Your Customer's Cash – John Mullins PhD and James Conlan

- Mastering the Rockefeller Habits: What You Must Do to Increase the Value of your Growing Firm – Verne Hamish

- Tao Te Ching: The New Translation from Tao Te Ching: The Definitive Edition (Tarcher Cornerstone Editions) – Lao Tzu

- Originals: How Non-Conformists Move the World – Adam Grant

- Zen Mind, Beginner's Mind: Informal Talks on Zen Meditation and Practice – Shuryu Suzuki

- Before Happiness; The 5 Hidden Keys to Achieving Success, Spreading Happiness and Sustaining Positive Change – Shawn Achor

- Essays in Idleness – Yoshida Kenko

- Daily Rituals: How Artists Work – Mason Currey

- Nassim Nicholas Taleb's complete works

- Tao of Jeet Kune Do – Bruce Lee

- "Circle of Influence" – Irvine, 2009

- How Will You Measure Your Life? – Christensen, Clayton M. HarperCollins.

- High Growth Handbook – Gil, Elad. (p. 109). Stripe Press.

- Tao Te Ching: A New English Version – Lao Tzu, Stephen Mitchell

- Life in Code: A Personal History of Technology – Ellen Ullman

- Factfulness: Ten Reasons We're Wrong About The World – And Things Are Better Than You Think – Hans Rosling, Ola Rosling, Anna Rosling Ronnlund

- The Founder's Dilemmas – Noam Wasserman

- The Republic – Plato

- YCombinator website

Made in the USA
Lexington, KY
29 October 2018